MagicImage Filmbooks
Presents

HOUSE OF FRANKENSTEIN

(The Original 1944 Shooting Script)

Edited
by
Philip J. Riley

Introduction by Peter Coe
An Interview with Elena Verdugo
Commentary by Glenn Strange
Production Background by Gregory Wm. Mank

Atlantic City · Hollywood

**UNIVERSAL FILMSCRIPTS SERIES
CLASSIC HORROR - VOLUME 6**

HOUSE OF FRANKENSTEIN
(The Original 1944 Shooting Script)

FIRST EDITION

Published by MagicImage Filmbooks, 740 S. 6th Avenue, Absecon, NJ 08201

Copyright © 1991, MagicImage Productions, Inc. All rights reserved.
Reproduction in whole or in part is prohibited without the written permission of the copyright holder.

Photographs, filmscript and other production materials used with the permission of and by special arrangement with Universal Studios.

The opinions expressed in this book are those of the individual authors and not the publisher.

The film HOUSE OF FRANKENSTEIN Copyright 1944 by Universal Pictures Company, Inc. Renewed 1970 by Universal Pictures.

This book contains the original shooting script by Edward T. Lowe, based on a story by Curt Siodmak

The Library of Congress Cataloging in Publication Data:

Lowe, Edward T.
   MagicImage Filmbooks presents House of Frankenstein : the original 1944 shooting script / edited by Philip J. Riley ; introduction by Peter Coe ; with commentary by Glenn Strange ; interview with Elena Verdugo; production background by Gregory Wm. Mank. -- 1st ed.
    p. cm. -- (Universal Filmscripts Series. Classic Horror films ; v. 6)
   "This book contains the original shooting script by Edward T. Lowe, based on a story by Curt Siodmak"--T.p. verso.
   ISBN 1-882127-17-X : $19.95
   1. House of Frankenstein (Motion picture) I. Riley, Philip J., 1948- . II. Siodmak, Curt, 1902- . III. MagicImage Filmbooks (Firm) IV. House of Frankenstein (Motion picture) V. Title. VI. Title: House of Frankenstein. VII. Series.
PN1997.H7113 1990
791.43'72--dc20   90-61039
                                                              CIP

This edition published in the USA by:
BearManor Media • 4700 Millenia Blvd. Suite 175 PMB 90497 • Orlando, Florida 32839
www.bearmanormedia.com

Hardcover: ISBN 978-1-62933-513-1
Paperback: ISBN 978-1-62933-512-4

    The purpose of this series is the preservation of the art of writing for the screen. Rare books have long been a source of enjoyment and an investment for the serious collector, and even in limited printings there usually were a few thousand produced. Scripts however, numbered only 50 at the most, and we are proud to present them in their original form. Some will be final shooting scripts and some earlier drafts, so that students, libraries, archives and film-lovers might, for the first time, study them in their original form. In producing these volumes, we hope that the unique art of screenplay writing will be preserved for future generations.

CREDITS AND ACKNOWLEDGMENTS

A Michael D. Stein Production

Editor, Philip J. Riley

Art Director, Marisa Donato-Riley

Artists, Robert Semler, A.S.I.
       Marisa Donato-Riley

Creative Consultant, Andrew Lee, Head of Research, Universal Studios (retired)

Editorial Assistant, Janet Stein

Cover - Courtesy Cinema Collectors, Hollywood, CA
Pressbook - Courtesy Richard Bojarski Collection

The editor wishes to thank the following individuals and institutions for their generous assistance:

Ronald V. Borst
James Cerone
Ned Comstock
Nancy Cushing-Jones
Sue Dwiggins
Rita Duenas
Donald Fowle
Eric Hoffman
Maria Jochsberger
Urbano Lemus

Linda Mehr
Lee Nesler
Norm Newberry
John Poorman
Anne Schlosser
Michael Sington
Dorothy Swerdlove
George Turner
Wallace Worsley

THE BILLY ROSE THEATER COLLECTION,
New York Public Library, Lincoln Ctr., New York City
THE MARGARET HERRICK LIBRARY,
Academy of Motion Picture Arts and Sciences
USC ARCHIVES OF PERFORMING ARTS,
SPECIAL COLLECTIONS

Manufactured in the United States of America

Typesetting by Computer House, Absecon, New Jersey

Printed and bound by
McNaughton & Gunn Lithographers

OTHER MAGICIMAGE PUBLICATIONS

THE ACKERMAN ARCHIVES SERIES
(Restoring Lost Films)
By Philip J. Riley

Volume 1 - LONDON AFTER MIDNIGHT
Volume 2 - A BLIND BARGAIN
Volume 3 - THE HUNCHBACK OF NOTRE DAME
Volume 4 - THE ROGUE SONG
Volume 5 - THE DIVINE WOMAN

. . . .

UNIVERSAL FILMSCRIPTS SERIES

Classic Horror Series
Volume 1 - FRANKENSTEIN
Volume 2 - THE BRIDE OF FRANKENSTEIN
Volume 3 - SON OF FRANKENSTEIN
Volume 4 - THE GHOST OF FRANKENSTEIN
Volume 5 - FRANKENSTEIN MEETS THE WOLF MAN
Volume 6 - HOUSE OF FRANKENSTEIN
Volume 7 - THE MUMMY
Volume 12- THE WOLFMAN
Volume 13- DRACULA

Classic Comedy Series
Volume 1 - ABBOTT AND COSTELLO MEET
                FRANKENSTEIN
Volume 2 - ONE NIGHT IN THE TROPICS
Volume 3 - BUCK PRIVATES
Volume 4 - HOLD THAT GHOST

Science Fiction Series
Volume 1 - THIS ISLAND EARTH
Volume 2 - CREATURE FROM THE BLACK LAGOON
Volume 3 - THE INVISIBLE MAN

Academy Award Series
Volume 1 - ALL QUIET ON THE WESTERN FRONT

Classic Silents Series
Volume 1 - THE PHANTOM OF THE OPERA (1925)

Classic Alfred Hitchcock
Volume 1 - PSYCHO

§ AUTOBIOGRAPHY §

The Wizard of MGM- 42 Years of Special Effects
   - By A. Arnold Gillespie
(Introduction by Katharine Hepburn and Spencer Tracy)

Mr. Technicolor - By Dr. Herbert Kalmus

. . . .

For ordering information, please call or write:

MagicImage Filmbooks
740 S. 6th Avenue
Absecon, NJ 08201
(609) 652-6500

Dedicated to:

The House of J.J. Cohen

(You will never see J.J. Cohen's name in relation to the motion picture business, but none of my works would ever have been accomplished without his support and confidence; and <u>all</u> of these most important historical documents might, in time, have turned to dust - thus leaving a whole chapter of unique American literature to tragically disappear, as have 50% of all motion pictures made in this century. - Ed.)

Introduction
by
Peter Coe

Although the subject of this book is one of my Universal horror films, *House of Frankenstein*, Philip Riley, the editor of these books, has related that the purpose of the series is to assure firsthand knowledge of old Hollywood rather than leaving the scandalous and speculative books that are so popular at present (and are usually written by people whose *parents* were not even born yet when the films were being made) as a misleading legacy for the children of the future.

And so as requested, I will tell you a little about myself.

Petar Knego (my real name) was born on November 11, 1918 in the small but famous resort town of Dubrovnik, Yugoslavia. At that time Yugoslavia was part of the Austro-Hungarian Empire and known as The Kingdom of Serbo-Croat and Slavicks. Yugoslavia and I were born on the same day! Armistice Day. That day the southern kingdom of Slavia became Jugoslavia (Jug - meaning south) - South Slavia.

During World War I, my father had been a captain in the Army. Before the war, going back generations, the whole family were sailors and merchant marines. I turned out to be an exception by going into the dramatic arts, which produced the expected result from a proud family of sea-farers - my father disowned me!

As far back as five years of age, I wrote plays, designed costumes, put on shows and charged admission. I remember falling in love with a famous German actress named Brigitte Helm. I fell in love with her when I saw her in Fritz Lang's *Metropolis* (UFA, 1926) which made her an international star. She had come to Dubrovnik to make a film with Anton Walbrook called *Der Zigeunerbaron* (The Gypsy Baron). Anton was a famous Austrian actor who a few years later fled Germany to escape the Nazi plague, and is best known today for the English film *The Red Shoes* (1947). I got to play my first film role in *The Gypsy Baron* as Walbrook's son, a young Gypsy boy.

After that experience I too went to England, and began my theatre training at the Royal Academy of Dramatic Arts. Aside from the theatre, another love of mine is swimming. My ancestors made a living on the water and I felt more at home *in* the water. In 1936 I won the British Empire Swimming Championship race, held in honor of the coronation of King Edward. (Not bad, considering that the American contestant was Johnny Weissmuller.) Sara Delano Roosevelt, the mother of American President FDR, had seen the race and made it possible for me to become a citizen of the United States.

To complete my training and learn the English language (I could speak five languages in my early school years) I attended the American School of Dramatic Arts. After graduation my first "show business" job was for Billy Rose in his Aquacade at the 1939 World's Fair as understudy to - Johnny Weissmuller.

Next stop, Broadway, in a play called "The Fifth Column," directed by Lee Strasberg. "My Sister Eileen" directed by George S. Kaufman followed. In "A Man in Shadow," I played a Nazi Lieutenant and received two major compliments - the first being hissed off the stage and the second attracting the attention of one of the biggest Hollywood agents, Charles K. Feldman. Feldman arranged for my transportation and my first screen test at Universal for Director Howard Hawks.

During the screen test I met the famous makeup artist Jack Pierce for the first time. He was so helpful and encouraging. Perhaps he knew that I was a new American citizen and he remembered the days when he had first emigrated from Greece. Hawks, however, became ill, and the picture was assigned to Director John Rawlins. Rawlins hated me. I hated the test and wanted to get on a train and go back to the theater world in New York City.

Fortunately the cinematographer on the test, Hal Mohr, kept up my spirits, as did my agent. Academy Award winning producer Walter Wanger (then at Universal) saw the test and liked it. He was about to begin a war picture, *Gung Ho*, and had a character written into the script especially for me; changed my name to Peter Coe; and the picture was a hit. Soon I was introduced to the Universal stars Abbott and Costello, Deanna Durbin, Gloria Jean, Allan Jones, Donald O'Connor and so many others. Nate Blumberg was in charge of the studio at that time. My next part was in a Universal "All-Star" review called *Follow the Boys*. It had a lot of outside players like Sophie Tucker, Jeanette MacDonald, Orson Welles, and Marlene Dietrich - all clients of my agent Charlie Feldman.

Maria Montez was the next to help me along. She had seen my old test and wanted me to play 'Tonio' the Gypsy in her next film, *Gypsy Wildcat*. The makeup in those early Universal 3-strip Technicolor films was so thick and the lights so hot that if you stood still for a few minutes the makeup would just melt off. But Natalie Kalmus, the representative from Technicolor, thought that I looked "beautiful" in color. I could have thought of a better adjective, but the compliment was nice. She would be there every day of the shooting to supervise the colors and costumes.

Director Roy William Neill (FRANKENSTEIN MEETS THE WOLF MAN, 1943) with Peter and Maria Montez in Universal's GYPSY WILDCAT, 1944.

I am sure, however, that for this volume of the Universal Filmscripts Series, you are more interested in my memories of *House of Frankenstein* and the other cast members.

I made two of Universal's horror films, back to back - *House of Frankenstein* and *The Mummy's Curse*. I'll save my stories of the Mummy film for Mr. Riley's future book on that title.

Jack Pierce was again the makeup artist. I was in awe of his talents. To me, he was the best makeup artist of his time, in Hollywood. Not only could he make the leading ladies at Universal beautiful, especially in the Technicolor films, but he also created all of the famous monsters. He didn't have much to do with me. Just brush on the pancake and that was it. The makeup was quite different on the set than how it photographed in the finished black and white films. Lon's makeup for the Wolf Man was brownish green hair, or whatever material was used, but his nose and cheeks were bright red. The Monster's skin was a greenish metallic color and Dracula also had a greenish tint to the white pancake.

Annie Gwynne and I were the lovers in the picture. We liked each other, but we kept our distance. Perhaps there was an attraction and we both felt it. She is a very nice girl.

George Zucco and Lionel Atwill were tough to work with, but only because I was in awe of them. I used to see them in films when I was a kid. Lionel was a wonderful man, a very strong personality outside, but I felt that he was a very sensitive man. The movie industry has always been an extremely tough world for good or sensitive people. To use the old phrase, 'They eat you up alive' if you are too kind or nice.

George filmed most of his scenes in just a few days, so I did not get much of a chance to watch him work.

Boris Karloff was an amazing man. He was not a young man when he first made his mark on film history as the Frankenstein Monster, and our film together was made 13 years later. There seemed times, between the scenes, when he looked very tired and he had trouble with his legs, but when the director called for action he would straighten up, and an inner energy force could be seen taking over his body. His eyes would just radiate and it looked as if he became 15 years younger to become the sinister, mad doctor while the cameras kept rolling. I got to know Boris from the theatre, for while I was performing on Broadway in "My Sister Eileen" he was starring in "Arsenic and Old Lace." In fact, this was one of his first pictures back at Universal and everyone treated him like a legend returned home.

John Carradine was a real character. We made a few pictures since that time, but my first impression of him was not the best. It was quite unsettling. To see this very thin, angular man dressed in his evening clothes and top hat, one would expect the personality to be different. But suddenly he spoke with a voice like Roosevelt. It boomed out of that body like a cannon and the Shakesperean intonations gave it a bite that hurt your ears.

Our first scene together took place on an old creepy, fog-shrouded dirt road. Annie and I and Sig Rumann, who played my grandfather, were walking home after visiting Boris' Horror caravan and a black carriage pulls up behind us and stops. We were not supposed to know that he was Count Dracula, who had just been accidentally but conveniently brought back to life by Boris who pulled the stake from his skeleton.

The carriage door opens and there is Carradine, who is supposed to step down out of the coach and say the line from the script, with 'old world politeness,' "If you are going to Riegelberg may I offer you the accommodation of my coach?"

Anne and Peter in another publicity shot with Universal's third Dracula, John Carradine.

The original script called for both Annie and I to be Americans, but with my accent it didn't seem to work. I was supposed to say something about "hitchhiking," and Dracula reacted with puzzlement at the unfamiliar American term. Remember this script was not written by Curt Siodmak; the story was his idea, but the script was written by someone else.

Well the cameras started rolling and the coach stops. The first thing that booms out of Carradine's mouth is, "I beg your pardon, but if you happen to be going my way, I'll be delighted to give you a lift." As soon as I heard that I knew that he had stolen the scene. I said to myself, "---- I'm gone! What am I going to do with this guy? He's going to eat us up! A Rumanian Vampire that sounds like a Shakesperean Taxi cab driver?" So I underplayed the remainder of the scene. When Erle Kenton called us in to see the rushes he said that we had a ham in our midst...a baked ham. Even Carradine had to admit it. Kenton says, "Guys we have to reshoot the whole bloody sequence. John, you were too high and Peter, you were too low." So John and I had a talk. "You know I had a little Broadway experience, Mr. Carradine, I didn't just walk in off the street." Then he broke down the pretense and smiled, "I did think that you were just a green kid." Now you must remember that John had his own Shakespearean company and he would usually take parts like this just to support his cast of loyal players. Sort of the same situation as Orson Welles. But when I said, "Are you going to be on the level with me or pull the same thing tomorrow?" he cracked up and respected me for that. So we played the scene as you see it in the final film and we became fairly good friends after that.

J. Carrol Naish and I had already done one picture together, and I remember on the *Frankenstein* set he gave me a piece of advice. He said,"You know, you're a good actor Peter, but you will sink on the screen." I thought he said stink, and was about to tell him what I thought of the movie caste system when he went on, "You have to use your eyes. Move your hands. That registers in the camera more than your voice, your speech, your looks." And then he drank down a full glass of water. In one long gulp. When he turned back to continue I realized that it wasn't water but booze! Now you can imagine what my adventures were like during the remaining time during shooting with Naish, Carradine and Lon and their unquenchable thirst. I thought to myself, My god! How do they do it! I must be missing something? So I started drinking with them. Talk about hell raising!

They even had a club called 'The Shin-Kicking Club.' All the guys at Universal, and some of them were big and rugged like Chaney and Brod Crawford, would meet at a bar called 'Fosters' near the studio. The whole idea was when a member greeted you with a less than 'big and rugged' greeting like "Hi, Luv," or "Hi Baby," it was swiftly followed by a hard kick in the shins. If you showed any pain or let out any choice words, you had to buy a round of drinks for everybody. Believe me, when a man the size of Chaney kicks you in the shins, you end up buying a lot of drinks.

Lon and I became good friends on that picture; a friendship that lasted almost 30 years until he passed away in 1973.

Lon was quite a guy. He and Patsy, his wife, had a nice home in the Valley that he called his "ranch." We had a break in shooting for the weekend in hunting season and Lon says, "Peter, how about you and me packing our gear and going up to the ranch in the Valley for the weekend?" I say "Sure Lon, what time do you want to pick me up?" Well, he says that he'll be by early in the morning and that I should bring some warm clothes since duck season had just opened and it might be cold. Now I'm used to New York cold, but cold in California was like the fall back east, so I dig out my hunting clothes and the next day I'm all packed and ready. What Lon forgot to tell me was that he had *another* ranch and it was about 600 miles north of Hollywood in Rice field just north of Sacramento in the *Sacramento* Valley!

We loaded up the car with provisions, a case of whiskey and we were off. The first bottle was gone before we even left the San Fernando Valley. I really don't know how we even made it to his cabin, but it took about 8 hours and we arrived about 9:30 or 10:00 at night. The shape we were in by that time, it's a wonder he didn't park the car in the living room.

But we made it into the cabin and went right to sleep. He had a caretaker up at the ranch who was going to be our guide. So about 2:30 or 3:00 - a.m.! - the guide arrived and Lon came over to my bed and started nudging me to wake me up saying, "Peter, Peter, wake up. Here's a glass." So I took the glass, thinking that it was tomato or orange juice, and started to drink. It was a water glass full of pure whiskey! Now that sobered me up quick. When I finished, Lon poured another one, "To keep the cold out," and then another "For a good day's hunt," and then another. Soon we were gone again and up we go on our hunting trip. When I think back about it all I can think is, 'My god, we could have shot each other,' easily.

But we didn't, and after a few hours we took a little rest. A short time later I looked up and the sky is dark. I said to myself, this can't be. Did we get so drunk that we slept all day? I looked at my watch and it is only 10 a.m., then I looked at Lon and said, "Lon what is that, what is going on?" He says, "Canadian Geese, the biggest flock I've ever seen. I think they are going to land." And by golly they did. They landed about a mile or a mile and a half away. He said, "Cm'on, Peter, we're going to get some of those babies." So there we were in the rice fields crawling on our bellies army style, and we finally got within range without them sensing us. I was a good shot and so was Lon. We opened fire and got real lucky. When the flock scattered I got up to gather our game, but Lon grabbed me by the arm and said,"Let's get, Peter, run." "Run? But Lon, we must have gotten 50 geese, that's what were here for isn't it?" "Not exactly," he said, " Those are geese, it's *duck* hunting season. " Yes? and...." I asked, "And do you know how many geese you're allowed shoot?" I shook my head and he held up one finger. "Each. Now let's get the hell out of here before the game warden finds us. We'll come back later." He didn't have to say another word. I was a half mile ahead of him before he could move, thinking, *Here I am with a seven year contract with Universal and I'm going to spend half of it in jail over a goose!* Well, 49 geese to be exact.

We did come back with a truck late at night and load them up, and we didn't wait for morning to head back to Hollywood. Back in Hollywood we ate geese, gave away geese, after a month we were sick of geese. We had a feast! Breaking the law like that is not something that I was proud of, but I wasn't about to give up a way of keeping the grocery bills down after all that effort.

Coe and Chaney in THE MUMMY'S CURSE, 1944

On the set at Universal, however, it was all business. Lon and I were working on *The Mummy's Curse* right after we completed *House of Frankenstein,* and Lon got mad at me because I wouldn't have a drink with him. I cussed at him and said, "Lon, you don't have a '--------' line to say. I have all the dialogue! You put on your mask and get wrapped in torn sheets and go 'Uhh, Grrr, Uhhh' while you extend one arm and shuffle around and walk into walls, I mean through walls. I've got all this dialogue to prepare! I won't drink on the set!" As big as he was he had a way of getting to you like a lost little kid. I was always a sucker for that look, and I told him that after the day's shoot was over I would join him for a drink. That brought a smile to his face.

Sometimes I think back and imagine that Lon and I secretly wanted to trade places. He always wanted to play the romantic leading man, and I could have used the break of a non-dialogue role.

There was one time that I was to be interviewed by Hedda Hopper. We were having a nice talk during lunch in the Universal commissary and the assistant director came over to us and said, "Oh Peter, we just wrote a new scene and we want you to shoot it right after lunch." I looked at it and almost fell on the floor! It wasn't a scene, it was 13 pages of soliloquy, solid, bloody dialogue!

When we got back on the set I showed it to Hedda and she said, "They've got to be kidding." I told her that they weren't; they meant it. I went to the assistant director and said, "No one can do this! You guys are crazy!"

Well, believe it or not, I did it. And they ended up using it as a montage sequence over some of the older Mummy films as a filler.

We had an actor, an older star named William Farnum, in the cast. The director on that film was Leslie Goodwins. Goodwins was a little Englishman, who later became a television director - set-em-up, shoot-em-up, and move on - no retakes. He really had no respect for this once very famous and popular star, who had been a leading man before the director was even born!

Bill, who must have been 80 years old in 1944, was having a horrible time remembering his lines and the director would berate him for holding up the shooting. Well, Lon turned to me and said, "This man was a friend of my dad's. He was a big star! This so-and-so isn't going to get away with this!" We marched down to the production office and told them, "Look! You get a star chair for Mr. Farnum with his name on it and treat him with the respect that he deserves!" The little man in the office didn't even bother to look up, and said, "Or?" Well Lon starts toward the door and says, "OR, Peter and I are not going back to work! And without us there's no picture and without the picture there's no need for a little s--- like you to take up space in a closed down production office!"

The next day Mr. Farnum has his chair. With his name on it. He finished his dialogue. He still stumbled with his lines, but he finished and everyone gave him a round of applause. He was so grateful that he had tears in his eyes. That was a beautiful thing that Lon had done. In fact, anything that reminded Lon of his father would touch a soft spot in his heart. He really loved his father. It wasn't at all like it was presented in the film about Sr. called *Man of a Thousand Faces* that was made about 10 years after *House of Frankenstein*. In fact the man who wrote that film was also a friend of mine, and one day I went to him and asked where he had gotten all that misinformation about Lon and his father. Bob Campbell was his name, and he said, "It was all in the archives!?" I told him that he should have gone to the man himself and talked to him about it. I don't think he realized that Lon was still around and he could have gotten the true story. Instead they went to Cleva, Lon's mother, and got the version that appeared on the screen. Cleva was around until the late 1960's.

Someday the real story about the Chaneys will be told, but I think that the motion pictures they collectively made are what is really important. A person's personal life has no place in history books.

My own story has a very happy ending. While I was in Yugoslavia in 1965 shooting a film called *The Secret Invasion*, in the midst of the cast, crew and technicians all running about, all of a sudden an old man appeared in the crowd. At first I just breezed past him with my eyes, but as he took one step toward me, away from the others I suddenly recognized him. Not a word was spoken as he moved closer to me and then I moved toward him and we hugged and embraced and kissed. It was my father, who had disowned me 28 years before and with whom I hadn't spoken through almost three decades. It was one of the most beautiful moments of my life. I never told that to Lon, for I believe that it was something that he had always wished he could have with *his* father. He loved his father dearly and never once spoke in a derogatory fashion about their relationship.

That is about all that I have to recall on my journey into Universal's "monsterland." Even though I made almost 75 films, it is nice to be a part of something that still has such a big following almost 50 years later.

Peter Coe
Santa Monica, California
January, 1991

Peter Coe has remained active in the motion picture industry ever since he left Universal and enlisted in the Marines in 1944. Upon his return to Hollywood he acted in major stock companies and playhouses on both coasts.

His credits since 1945 include: Sands of Iwo Jima, Can Can, Tobruk, The Prize, Diplomatic Courier, Vigilante Force, The Road to Bali, The Egyptian, The 10 Commandments, The Buccaneer, Okeefenokee, Hellgate, Rocky Mountain and Secret Invasion. His last film was Vigilante Force in 1976.

He has been active in television, teaching, directing and producing ever since, and today lives happily with his fourth wife Tomasa, and has six children by previous marriages: Diane from his first, Dana from his second, three sons by his third marriage to Roselle Calvert (a famous 1950's era New York high-fashion model), and is very proud of his youngest son, Peter, a successful record producer living in Hollywood.

He is always around for his life-long friends like Robert Mitchum and others when they need advice on a part, but is hesitant to take on students unless they show exceptional talent.

Universal Studios honors its past stars, celebrities, directors and technicians every year by a reunion party during the fall months. They report that one of the most popular guests each year has been Peter Coe.

An Interview with Elena Verdugo
by
Gregory Wm. Mank

"...a werewolf doesn't just die. He must be killed - killed by a silver bullet - fired by the hand of one who loves him enough to understand..."
— Universal folklore
from *House of Frankenstein*

"All theatre-goers like to 'hiss' the villain. Instead of only ONE villain to hiss, *House of Frankenstein* has FIVE....Conduct a 'HISS THE VILLAIN CONTEST' in your lobby....Set up a regulation ballot-box....Carry this banner copy across the top: 'HISS THE VILLAIN CONTEST...VOTE FOR THE HORROR CHARACTER YOU HATE THE MOST!'"

So proclaimed the pressbook when Universal's five-ring circus of terror, *House of Frankenstein*, premiered in December of 1944. What villain would be "hated the most" by the disciples of melodrama who flocked to the film? Would it be Boris Karloff's mad, vengeance-crazed Dr. Niemann? Lon Chaney's tragic Lycanthrope Larry Talbot? John Carradine's spidery Count Dracula? J. Carrol Naish's lovesick, psychotic hunchback, Daniel? Glenn Strange's Frankenstein Monster?

Meanwhile, cavorting through this 70-minute "Monster Rally" providing relief from the villains, yet supplying some of the movie's most dramatic moments, was the leading lady: the tragic Gypsy girl Ilonka, played zestfully, emotionally and so memorably by Elena Verdugo.

In the course of *House of Frankenstein*, Miss Verdugo's spirited Ilonka performed a festive Gypsy dance, flirted with Naish's Daniel, fell in love with Chaney's Talbot, exploded in hysterics at the news her love was a Lycanthrope, screamed wildly as she lovingly ended the Wolf Man's sufferings with a silver bullet, and, climactically, played a lush, almost operatic death scene - crawling through the misty forest to the body of Larry Talbot, to die with her head resting peacefully on his chest.

It was all a wild dramatic showcase for Miss Verdugo, who reached her 19th birthday during the shooting of *House of Frankenstein* - but already she was a seasoned performer. She had been dancing since she was a small child, had made her movie debut in *Down Argentine Way* (1940), and had attracted notice as George Sanders' native girl love in *The Moon and Sixpence* (United Artists, 1942). Later, she would enjoy movie adventures with Charlie Chan and Gene Autry, become the star of the CBS comedy series *Meet Millie* (1952-1956) and, 25 years after *House of Frankenstein*, return to Universal City to play Nurse Consuelo Lopez in ABC's long-running *Marcus Welby, M.D.*

Today, Elena Verdugo is retired, living in Baja, Mexico with her husband, Dr. Charles Rosewall. As striking as ever, the actress graciously gave this interview about her Monster Rally of over 40 years ago:

Q. "Vivacious Elena Verdugo had the unusual experience of working for the first time upon soil that once belonged to her forefathers.....," reports the pressbook for *House of Frankenstein*. True?

A. It's true. Much of North Hollywood, Studio City, Burbank and Universal City was the original Spanish land grant to Jose Maria Verdugo, a soldier in the Spanish army. I once got a laugh when I reminded an irritating director at Universal that he was standing on my property!

I was not under contract to Universal. The main condition for it had been for me to lose weight, and I rebelled. But I played more pictures for them than did many of the studio's contract players, and *House of Frankenstein* was my debut there.

Q. Already, you were an experienced performer?

A. I was a local L.A. girl, and had been a dancer from age five. Movies were work, not glamour. Almost all of my family were in some area of film or music locally. My mother usually took me to the set, and then I went home to my family and old neighborhood.

Q. Your talent as a dancer, as well as beauty and dramatic energy, won you the role of Gypsy dancer Ilonka. However, you're blonde - and Universal couldn't accept a blonde Gypsy girl.

A. As Ilonka, I used a brunette wig. In fact, I had to wear a wig in several pictures until I escaped those "Gypsy" roles and played Lou Costello's girl in *Little Giant* (Universal, 1946). Sometimes dye was used instead of a wig. An industry joke was that I was Hollywood's only light-at-the-roots brunette!

Q. What was it like, working with the stars of *House of Frankenstein*?

A. Working with Boris Karloff, I had an intense awareness that I was working with a "great." He was a serious actor, but never unkind. Lon Chaney was a lovely, friendly man. I remember often sitting and chatting with him. I had met J. Carrol Naish on the set of my first picture, *Down Argentine Way* (20th Century-Fox, 1940), when I was 15. He loved working. I simply loved him. He helped, he supported, he gave so much. I'd see Glenn Strange in the makeup department every a.m. Glenn was dear, and Jack Pierce, his makeup man, was a genius.

Q. Your Gypsy dance, which introduces you in *House of Frankenstein*, comprises over a minute-and-a-half of screen time. Was it your own creation?

A. I had to choreograph the Gypsy dance carefully myself. It was difficult, because at the last moment I learned that it was to be done on a slope that had not even been cleared of rocks.

Q. I understand that, for all the fun in making the movie, there was one wig-raising experience?

A. For the horror films at Universal, they used to have professional screamers on the sets. For the scene in which the Wolf Man attacked me, they called one of those "screamers" to our stage...I hadn't seen Lon in his makeup. Well, when the Wolf Man jumped out at me, I was so scared and screamed so wildly that they cancelled the professional screamer!

All in all, I enjoyed making the picture very much. I was a still-growing teenage girl, and ALL those fine actors were kind, considerate, and made me feel a part of everything.

With Lou Costello in LITTLE GIANT (1946)

Production Background
By
Gregory Wm. Mank

Boris Karloff as Jonathan Brewster in "Arsenic and Old Lace", 1944.

Early in 1944, there was joy and jubilation at Universal City: Boris Karloff was back on his Coldwater Canyon farm, high in the mountains above Beverly Hills. The legendary star of *Frankenstein, The Mummy, The Old Dark House, The Black Cat, The Bride of Frankenstein, Son of Frankenstein* and so many Universal nightmares had returned after a year-and-a-half in the Broadway cast of *Arsenic and Old Lace*, followed by a 66-week national tour of the play. All in all, Karloff had tallied over 1,000 performances as mad Jonathan Brewster - who killed one victim because, "He said I looked like Boris Karloff."

To celebrate the return of Karloff, Universal overtured the actor with a deluxe star contract - and envisioned the ultimate in Universal horror.

Meanwhile, Boris Karloff signed his Universal star contract. The deal had to proceed like clockwork: Karloff would engage his services to Universal for 13 weeks; he would work 12 of those weeks at $5,000 per week; and in that period, he would star in two pictures. On February 1, 1944, Karloff began working the first eight weeks (and earning the first $40,000) in *The Climax*; producer George Waggner dusted off this old chestnut, had Curt Siodmak revamp the story, reopened the Paris Opera House on Soundstage 28 (where he had produced the sumptuous 1943 *Phantom Of The Opera*, which would win two Oscars), and added Technicolor and beautiful, blonde soprano Susanna Foster - all on a $750,000 budget. Paul Malvern, veteran "B" Western producer who was enjoying new prestige following the success of his Maria Montez/Jon Hall Technicolor *Ali Baba and the Forty Thieves*, was entrusted with the "other" Karloff project - for which Boris would work his final four weeks, and receive the additional $20,000.

Screenwriter Curt Siodmak wrote the original story on which Edmund T. Lowe based his shooting script.

Among the writers at Universal, there was a game we played regarding the Monster. If you got the assignment of writing a Frankenstein picture, you always killed the Monster in such a way that nobody could survive it. You'd reduce him to cinders or ashes, so the next guy who had to write a Frankenstein film couldn't revive him. But then, there was always another picture, and somebody had to find a way of putting the Monster together again.

- Curt Siodmak

George Waggner and crew setting up a shot for THE PHANTOM OF THE OPERA, 1943.

The watery climax of *Frankenstein Meets The Wolf Man* pleased Curt Siodmak. The great flood unleashed by the exploding dam, rampaging through the castle ruins and washing away the battling horrors, seemed to the film's writer a definitive way of ridding the cinema world of the Monster and the Wolf Man. Siodmak certainly did not envy the writer who got the job of resurrecting the creatures once again.

Ironically, Siodmak got the job! A year after the release of *Frankenstein Meets the Wolf Man*, Universal assigned Siodmak to concoct a super horror epic to welcome Karloff back to the fold, a big parade of favorite Universal goblins. Not only were the waterlogged Monster and Wolf Man to be revived, but also Dracula and the Mummy (who, in the swathed form of Lon Chaney Jr., had most recently waddled into a backlot swamp, lugging "reincarnated love" Ramsay Ames in *The Mummy's Ghost*). Universal was determined to retain its horror supremacy, against such intended usurpers as RKO, where Val Lewton was producing such sublime chillers as *Cat People* (1942), *I Walked With a Zombie* (1943) and *The Seventh Victim* (1943).

In the fascinating study entitled Universal Horrors, The Studio's Classic Films, 1931-1946 (McFarland & Company, Inc., 1990), Michael & John Brunas and co-author Tom Weaver reveal the beginnings of *House of Frankenstein*:

"On June 7, 1943, The Hollywood Reporter announced that Universal was developing a new shocker entitled *Chamber of Horrors* with an all-star cast of ghouls including the Invisible Man, the Mad Ghoul, the Mummy and "other assorted monsters." George Waggner was named as the ringleader of this three-ring circus of horrors. The cast read like a Who's Who of cinemacabre: Karloff, Chaney, Lugosi, Lorre, Rains, Zucco, Hull and . . James Barton(?!)"

The original March 10, 1944 script (featured in this volume) is titled *Destiny*; the March 23, 1944 revision was entitled *The Devil's Brood*. As things evolved, Curt Siodmak wrote only the story for the film, which cleverly presented the

"THE DEVIL'S BROOD"

Prod. Title   Prod. No.

PART	ARTIST	From	To	Time	Rate	o	AMOUNT
CONTRACENT:							
Larry	Lon Chaney				FLAT	10T	10,000.
Rita	Anne Gwynne				FLAT	3T	3,000.
Carl	Peter Coe				FLAT	3T	3,500.
OUTSIDENT:							
Niemann	Boris Karloff	4/4	5/1	4	5,000.	200.	20,000.
Daniel	J. Carrol Naish	4/4	5/1	4	1,750.	50.	7,000.
Monster	Glen Strenge	4/12	4/25	2	250.	50.	500.
Dracula	John Carridine	4/26	5/9	2	3,500.	00.	7,000.
Hussman	Sig Rumann	4/27	5/6	1½	1,000.	00.	1,500.
Arnz	Lionel Atwill	4/26	5/2	1	1,750.	50.	1,750.
Toberman		4/20	4/26	1	500.	00.	500.
Muller		4/20	4/26	1	500.	00.	500.
Hertz		4/20	4/26	1	350.	00.	350.
Lampini	Geo. Zucco	4/6	4/12	1	1,500.	00.	1,500.
Meier		4/20	4/26	1	250.	00.	250.
Schwart		4/20	4/26	1	250.	00.	250.
Born		4/20	4/26	1	250.	00.	250.
Ilonka	Elena Verdugo	4/5	4/25	3	250.	00.	750.
ALLOW FOR WEEKLY STANDINS							400.
ALLOW FOR OVERTIME - WEEKLY PLAYERS							600.
DAYERS AS PER DETAIL ATTACHED							3,700.
807 - TO						6.	63,300.

Producer Paul Malvern presented Universal with this budget for casting.

Lon Chaney Jr. and silent film actor William Farnum welcome Boris Karloff back to Universal in 1944.

various ghouls via a travelling Chamber of Horrors, pirated by mad Dr. Gustav Niemann and his pathetic, psychotic hunchbacked assistant, Daniel. Edward T. Lowe wrote the actual screenplay. The men conservatively decided to drop the Mummy, "Kharis," that shuffling one-eyed creature whom Chaney had been playing with loud protests against the makeup.

Producer Malvern blueprinted the production. The total budget (including 25% studio overhead) came to $354,000; the shooting schedule was 30 days. Set to direct was Universal's Erle C. Kenton (1896 - 1980), who had helmed *The Ghost of Frankenstein*, and who signed on for this "Monster Rally" at a fee of $15,000.

Kenton is best remembered for three Abbott & Costello comedies for Universal - *Pardon My Sarong*, *Who Done It?* (1942) and *It Ain't Hay* (1943) - and the horror films *Island of Lost Souls* (Paramount, 1932), *The Ghost of Frankenstein* (1942), *House of Frankenstein* (1944), *House of Dracula* (1945), and *The Cat Creeps* (1946), all for Universal. He was born in Norboro, Montana on August 1, 1896. He began his career in Hollywood with the Mack Sennett Company in 1914 doing everything from carpentry to editing. By 1919 he was directing 2-reel comedies, and after two co-directing jobs he directed his first feature in 1920. He continued making films until 1950 and then switched to television, his best known series being *Racket Squad*, *Public Defender* and *The Texan*. His last television credit was in 1962. He died in 1980.

The budget afforded John P. Fulton $12,500 to create the movie's special effects, while allotting $3,000 for the "makeup and hairdressing" necessary for not one but five horrific characters. Production would have to proceed virtually by stopwatch: Karloff, per his contract, was to work only the first four weeks, the time he owed Universal; the last week of shooting would be devoted to the Dracula episode, in which Niemann hardly appeared.

Presented to Karloff was the pivotal role of the crazed Niemann; although the actor was willing to return to the *Frankenstein* series, he was not about to break his vow never again to play his beloved Monster (whom he had so classically portrayed in *Frankenstein*, *The Bride of Frankenstein* and *Son of Frankenstein*). As Boris told the studio publicity department:

Horror implies abhorrence, aversion and repugnance. Terror makes your hair stand on end. I don't play roles that are revolting or repulsive. Nor is...my new picture revolting or repulsive, though it is certainly destined to take the curl out of anyone's hair.

Sharing star billing with Karloff was Lon Chaney, who, as a Universal contractee, would receive a flat $10,000 for *The Devil's Brood*. Chaney was rather bitter at this time; the studio had promised him his father's role in the remake of *Phantom of the Opera*, and then signed Claude Rains for the part. Still, Chaney was happy with *The Devil's Brood*. He was pleased to

Boris Karloff as Dr. Niemann

play his "baby," the Wolf Man, for a third time, and he was proud that the script fashioned Larry Talbot a love affair with Ilonka, the Gypsy girl. Chaney had not yet given up his campaign to become a screen heart throb.

Originally, Universal inferred that Bela Lugosi would don the cape of Dracula (no problem for wardrobe, as Lugosi owned and cherished several such capes). Lugosi very much wanted the part; he had frothed when the studio starred Chaney in 1943's *Son of Dracula*. However, the aging Lugosi sadly saw himself passed over by Universal, for reasons ranging from his poor health to the studio's lingering displeasure over his disastrous performance as the Monster in *Frankenstein Meets the Wolf Man*.

So Universal awarded the role of the Count to John Carradine (1906 - 1988). Carradine was now so infamous a Hollywood villain that, while riding in a movie star parade, he was booed and pelted with trash along the two-mile route. Laureled for his performances in such John Ford classics as 1936's *The Prisoner of Shark Island* (as vicious Sgt. Rankin), 1939's *Stagecoach* (as the mysterious gambler Hatfield) and 1940's *The Grapes of Wrath* (unforgettable as the martyr Casy), the cadaverous Carradine, 38, had also reigned from 1936 - 1942 as the skunk supreme of 20th Century-Fox (where, as Bob Ford in 1939's *Jesse James*, he committed his worst atrocity - shooting Tyrone Power in the back). Now Carradine was the producer, director, star and sole owner of his own repertory company, "John Carradine and his Shakespeare Players," touring the West Coast as Hamlet, Shylock and (alternately) Othello and Iago. As he declaimed to the New York Herald Tribune:

"I am a HAM! And the ham in an actor is what makes him interesting....I am the only actor I know who is equipped at this time to play classical repertory. While in Hollywood, I have kept up in all the roles - why I could go on stage in any Shakespearean part with only 24 hours' notice...I know Shakespeare practically by heart..."

Lon Chaney Jr. as Larry Talbot

John Carradine as Count Dracula (Baron Latos)

Carradine gallantly financed the company via such films as Monogram's *Voodoo Man* (as Lugosi's idiot helper Toby, stroking the hair of the female zombies) and Universal's *The Mummy's Ghost* (as high priest Yousef Bey of Karnak, tending to Chaney's crumbling Kharis). Eccentric, Carradine was one of the most picturesque inhabitants of the legendary "Garden of Allah," where he resided with his "Ophelia," voluptuously blonde Sonia Sorel. (They later married, hence Keith, Christopher and Robert Carradine.) According to Sheliah Graham's book, The Garden of Allah, Allah survivors still remember the night when Carradine announced (after some excellent Scotch) that he was the Christ, and would prove it by walking across the swimming pool. His neighbors left their villas, congregated poolside, and made bets as to whether or not Carradine was truly divine. He was not.

Anne Gwynne & Peter Coe as Rita & Carl Hussman

Carradine and his wife Sonia at the Garden of Allah

Signed for four weeks for the "sensation," and promised special billing in the bargain, was J. Carrol Naish (1897 - 1973). Like Carradine, the 47-year old Naish (who, for all his expertise at playing Indians, Mexicans and Italians, was actually of Irish ancestry) was one of Hollywood's best paid and busiest character men. His credits ranged from low budget potboilers such as *The Monster Maker* (which he had just finished at PRC) to Columbia's epic *Sahara* (for which he had just won an Academy Award nomination as the self-sacrificing Italian soldier) and Columbia's 1943 *Batman* serial (in which he played Oriental super-villain Dr. Daka).

Excellent players filled the supporting ranks. The irrepressible Lionel Atwill (1885 - 1946), now seriously romancing a 27-year old radio producer/singer named Paula Pruter (she became his fourth wife in July, 1944), happily accepted the role of Inspector Arnz.

George Zucco (1886 - 1960), that superb British screen menace with a funereal voice, here made his only Frankenstein film appearance as Professor Bruno Lampini, original proprietor of the Chamber of Horrors.

The lovely Anne Gwynne, Universal's "TNT girl" ("trim, neat, terrific"), was cast as Rita, Dracula's intended victim. Already a survivor of such studio melodramas as 1940's *Black Friday*, 1941's *The Black Cat* and 1944's *Weird Woman*, the copper-haired Miss Gwynne was the lot's No. 2 horror girl, never really anxious to try harder than her good friend Evelyn Ankers.

Peter Coe, a young studio contractee, took the part of Karl Hussman, Rita's bridegroom. And for the doomed Ilonka, Larry Talbot's gypsy romance, Universal signed the lovely, vivacious, teenage starlet, Elena Verdugo.

But what of the Monster?

Elena Verdugo as Ilonka, the Gypsy girl

J. Carrol Naish as Daniel, the hunchback

Lionel Atwill as Inspector Arnz

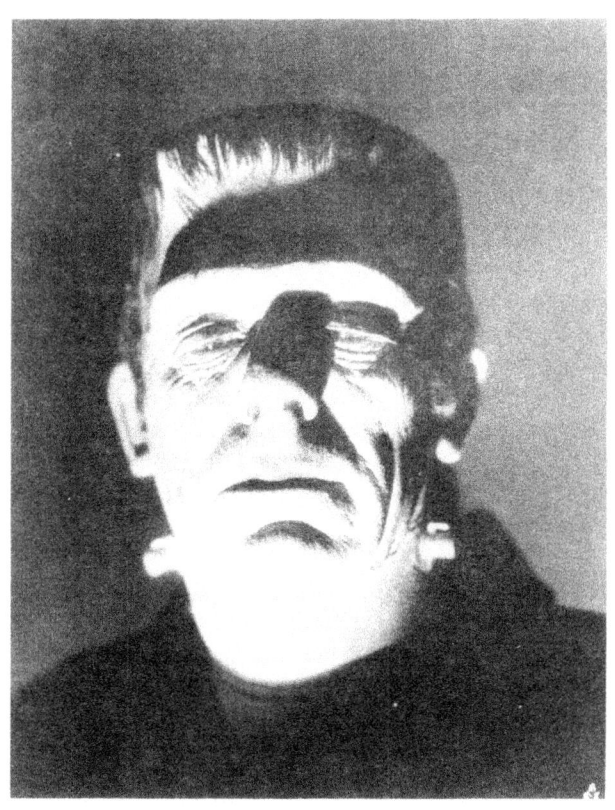

Glenn Strange as The Monster

George Zucco as Professor Bruno Lampini

During the 1931 Christmas season, Glenn Strange, 32-year old boxer, wrestler, rodeo performer and movie stunt man/bit player, went with his brother Virgil to see *Frankenstein* in El Paso, Texas. As they left the theatre, Virgil turned to his brother and said, "You know they can't build a guy up like that and make him breathe again. But where the hell did they ever find a guy that looked like THAT?"

Glenn Strange had just worked with the "guy" in Columbia's *The Guilty Conviction*. And although the six-feet-four, 218-pound "Peewee" (as he was called by his pals) devoted his major energies over the next 12 years to his family, nightclub brawls, comic books, and scores of "B" Westerns, screen horror seemed to loom in his destiny. In Universal's original 1936 *Flash Gordon* serial, Strange had played three parts: a robot of Ming the Merciless, a soldier of the Emperor, and a reptilian creature ("The Gocko" of the comics) that snared Flash in lobster-like pincers. In PRC's execrable *The Mad Monster* of 1942, Strange was the title terror, a hairy horror who, save for the fangs, was a dead ringer for Gabby Hayes. He had played a bit in *The Mummy's Tomb* (1942), and was featured in PRC's *The Black Raven* (1943) and *The Monster Maker* (1944).

Strange had no idea that Universal was seeking a new actor to play the Monster the morning he reported to Jack Pierce's studio to receive a facial scar. Nor was he aware that fellow Western heavy Lane Chandler had already made a test for the part. While Strange reclined in the makeup chair, Pierce suddenly excused himself, called Paul Malvern on the telephone, and told the producer that he had found the Monster.

Truly, Strange was just what Universal wanted. He was big, he was strong, he was prunefaced, he required no muscle padding, and (unlike the aging Bela Lugosi, who had played the Monster in 1943's *Frankenstein Meets the Wolf Man*), he wouldn't need a double. The 44-year old Strange was also in no position to demand the high salaries and lofty billing promised Karloff, Chaney, Naish and Carradine. The fourth actor to play Universal's Frankenstein Monster signed for only two weeks at $250 per week - and received no featured billing on the movie's posters or opening credits.

Meanwhile, as the shooting date neared, Joseph I. Breen, Hollywood's almighty censor, sent Universal a list of warnings about *The Devil's Brood*:

...We urge you to avoid all unnecessary gruesomeness, brutality, or horror in accordance with the requirements of the code...

All scenes of strangling should be handled with care; otherwise, they may be deleted by political censor boards...

Please avoid any undue gruesomeness as to the SOUND of Lampini's "choking cry and dying groan"...

Please have in mind...that the action of the villagers crossing themselves be not overemphasized...

Please exercise your usual good taste, in the scenes of Ilonka, to avoid any unacceptable movements in her dance...

Strange with Forrest J Ackerman, 1973

Universal had carefully budgeted the Special Effects: for fog, $1,000; for rain and lightning, $300; for the effect of the Monster and Wolf Man frozen in the cavern ice, $750; for the Dracula bat, $100....

On April Fool's Day, 1944, George Waggner completed *The Climax*. Karloff was free for picture #2. Universal had exactly four weeks to complete Karloff's work on *The Devil's Brood* - and the production was all set, and waiting in the wings.

A movie monster can get the wits scared out of him, the same as humans. He can get cold and hungry and tired. He can be insulted, and have his feelings hurt because people don't want to be in his company.

- Glenn Strange

The first day of shooting on *The Devil's Brood* was Tuesday, April 4, 1944. The company took full advantage of Universal's grand old sets. The stormy opening, showing Karloff and Naish in the dungeon, took place in the prison left over from James Whale's *Green Hell* (1940). After lightning struck, the psychotic pair escaped through tunnels - remains from the John Wayne/Marlene Dietrich/Randolph Scott *Pittsburgh* (1942). Meanwhile, out in the storm, Lampini's wagon was passing "Neustadt Prison" - actually Universal's set from 1939's *Tower of London*!

It would be a happy set. John Carradine now and then treated the company to his recitations of Shakespeare, and Lon Chaney, who loved to cook, sometimes prepared a lavish lunch in his dressing room for his co-stars. However, for Glenn Strange, there were many rude awakenings as he took on the role of the Monster. There was, of course, the three-and-a-half hour makeup adventure each day with Jack P. Pierce, his assistant Otto Lederer - and the side effects.

MOTION PICTURE PRODUCERS & DISTRIBUTORS OF AMERICA, INC.

HOLLYWOOD, CALIFORNIA

March 27, 1944

Mr. Maurice Pivar
Universal Pictures
Universal City, Calif.

Dear Mr. Pivar:

We have read the script, dated March 23, 1944, for your production THE DEVIL'S BROOD (formerly DESTINY), and are happy to report that the basic story seems to meet the requirements of the Production Code.

However, we call your attention to the following details:

We urge you strongly to avoid all unnecessary gruesomeness, brutality, or horror in accordance with the requirements of the Code.

Page 2: All scenes of strangling should be handled with care; otherwise, they may be deleted by political censor boards. In this connection, note also pages 3, 64, and 119.

Page 14: Please avoid any undue gruesomeness as to the sound of Lampini's "choking cry and dying groan." See also page 91.

Page 23: Please have in mind our previous request that the action of the villagers crossing themselves be not overemphasized.

Page 48 et seq: In these scenes of the horses being whipped and plunging along the road, we must ask that you consult with Mr. Craven, in accordance with our agreement.

Pages 57 & 59: Please exercise your usual good taste, in the scenes of Ilonka, to avoid any unacceptable movements in her dance.

Pages 63 & 64: Fejos' swinging the butt of his whip at Ilonka's head, and the lashings by Fejos and Daniel, should be indicated out of scene.

Page 98: Please avoid any undue gruesomeness and brutality as to scenes 319, 320, and 321.

Page 121: Any brutal details in scenes 424 & 425 should be masked.

You understand, of course, that our final judgment will be based on the finished picture.

Cordially yours,

cc: Mr. Work
    Mr. Murphy
    Mr. Kelley
    Mr. Bole
    Mr. J. Gershenson
    Mr. P. Malvern

Joseph I. Breen

The censor, Joseph Breen's letter to Universal after reviewing the script of THE DEVIL'S BROOD.

When I had the Monster makeup on, I used to have trouble seeing because the Monster's eyelids hung over my eyes. The makeup made my face raw, and lots of times I felt like I had water on the brain. You see, the skull cap I wore was so tight, it wouldn't let the perspiration out. So, after a couple of hours on the set, I could shake my head and the water would rattle around inside the skull cap.

- Glenn Strange

Strange discovered that playing a Monster created social repercussions, too:

I wasn't allowed in the studio commissary. I guess they didn't want me turning the stomachs of the stars and starlets. They brought me my lunch in a paper sack and I had to eat it where nobody could see me!

Still, for all the misadventures, Strange loved the engagement. For, in playing the Monster, he had the help of Karloff himself, whom Strange saluted as "...the greatest man in show business." Although Karloff was ill at the time with serious back trouble, drinking a quart of milk a day and nibbling crackers to try to gain weight, he was happy to help.

I'd never have been the Monster I was if it hadn't been for Boris Karloff. I remember, for instance, that he was sick during some of the filming. He had finished his scenes and could have gone home, but he stayed on and worked with me. He showed me how to make the Monster's moves properly, and how to do the walk that makes the Monster so frightening...

Ever since *Frankenstein*, the Universal series all seemed to have bizarre accidents on the sets, often becoming melodramas themselves. *House of Frankenstein* would be no exception.

On Wednesday, April 12, 1944, the company moved into Stage 17, to the interior of Niemann's laboratory, full of Kenneth Strickfaden's electrical wizardry - a $3,000 set. In one sequence there, Niemann supposedly thawed the Monster's tissues with steam as the creature lay in a large glass case. Strange would wince whenever he recalled how this glass case very nearly became his coffin:

The prop men pumped vapor into the box to make it look like steam. But I couldn't breathe, on account of the prop steam, so they put long rubber hoses in my nose so I could get air.

I was scared even before they put me in that thing. I told them, "now don't strap me down, cause if anything goes wrong, I want to GET OUT QUICK!"

Sympathetic, the prop crew installed a panic button inside the case. If Strange thought himself in danger, he could push this button and a red light would flash. Unfortunately, nobody was told to keep an eye on the light.

Sure enough, something went wrong. The hoses were so long, I couldn't breathe out the bad air and I was starting to suffocate. I laid on the panic button they gave me to push if anything happened, and that red cue light was flashing like the Fourth of July. Believe me, I almost died before somebody saw the light and got me out of there.

One of the worst accidents on the set did not victimize Strange; it was, to his great regret, caused by him. For the scene where the Monster threw Daniel through the window, the prop crew had placed plush mattresses behind the set upon which Naish (or more likely his double, Billy Jones) could comfortably land. "As I mentioned, it was hard for me to see with the Monster makeup on," said Strange, who misjudged his aim. The "hunchback" crashed through the breakaway window, missed the mattresses completely - and landed smack on the cement soundstage floor.*

On the night of Thursday, April 20, 1944 (Elena Verdugo's birthday), cast, crew and 45 extras beheld a magnificent stunt as Billy Jones performed the "exterior" action of Daniel's demise - rolling down the roof of "Niemann's castle" (actually Universal's Tower of London) and falling 30 feet into the net/mattresses out of camera range.

The big night was Monday, April 24, 1944. The company, plus an extra camera crew, filmed the fiery climax on the back lot, as Strange's Monster lugged Karloff's Niemann into the swamps, pursued by the torch-waving villagers. It was a rough night for Glenn Strange. While carrying Karloff's double, Carey Loftin, under his arm, Strange almost fell down 40 steep castle steps when an overly excited "villager" threw his heavy torch - and hit Strange in the back.

As the night wore on, Strange entered the back lot swamp, left over from Universal's *Nagana* (1933). As the villagers attacked with their torches, the swamp exploded into flames more violently than the Special Effects crew had planned. The flames singed Loftin's hair, and Strange galumphed much faster than he was directed into the safety of the quicksands.

Come 3:00 a.m., Kenton and crew shot the final scene - Niemann sinking into the quicksand with the Monster. For this close-up, Karloff naturally couldn't rely on double Carey Loftin. So, the distinguished star splashed into the goo, along with Strange, took a deep breath, and went under the muck and mire for the final fade-out shot. Following this 14-hour day, Karloff was back on the set the next afternoon, on time, for a scene in the Ice Caverns - and that night, hosted his radio show, "Creeps By Night!"

Although the quicksand scene completed Strange's work on the movie, Universal gratefully carried the trouper for an extra week on the payroll. At 4:30 p.m., Saturday, April 29, 1944, Karloff completed his work on the picture, right on schedule, on the Midnight Horror Show set; Naish finished his work that same afternoon, with Carradine, Anne Gwynne, Peter Coe, Lionel Atwill, Sig Rumann and 20 extras all on the set that day. Kenton turned his attention to the Dracula vignette, primarily saved for the last week of production.

---

* The scream, incidentally, that accompanies Naish's fall from the castle roof, is the same scream that Karloff unleashed in *Son of Frankenstein* when he discovered Lugosi's slain Ygor! So impressed was Universal by Karloff's howl that the studio re-recorded it and added the scream to the sound effects library. It was utilized, for example, in the 1944 Sherlock Holmes mystery, *The Spider Woman*.

On Saturday, May 6, Kenton took eight men and his crew to Sherwood Forest, far west in the San Fernando Valley near Malibu Beach, one hour from Universal City, to shoot the chase scene of the gendarmes pursuing Dracula's carriage over stream and hills. (Lake Sherwood, incidentally, is where Karloff's Monster tossed Little Maria in the 1931 *Frankenstein*.) At 8:00 a.m., Monday, May 8, John Carradine, Anne Gwynne and Peter Coe left Universal for Sherwood Forest, to complete the sequence.

At 5:00 that afternoon, in Sherwood Forest, Erle C. Kenton completed *The Devil's Brood* - exactly on the 30-day schedule.

The Devil's Brood itself became trapped in a studio bog, waiting over 7 months before playing its first engagements. In the meantime, Hans J. Salter again contributed a splendid score, dominated by gypsy themes, and Universal changed the title to the more commercial *House of Frankenstein*.

On Friday, December 15, 1944, *House of Frankenstein* opened at New York City's horror salon, the Rialto. On Friday, December 22, 1944, "The Greatest Shock Show the World Has Ever Seen!" opened at Hollywood's 956-seat Hawaii Theatre, supported on a double bill by Universal's *The Mummy's Curse* with Lon Chaney and Virginia Christine.

The Hollywood Citizen-News reported: "One very clever touch to his performance. When Strange's Monster awakes after 100,000 megavolts and sees Daniel, he laughs at him - obviously amused by the little hunchback's deformity. It is a cruel, ironic touch, one more suggestive of James Whale than Erle C. Kenton."

Karloff is a fine ringmaster for the circus of terrors in *House of Frankenstein*, flashing his eyes and milking such dialogue as "The undying Monster - the triumphant climax of Frankenstein's genius!" Chaney again possesses that strange magnetism as the cursed Talbot (he would play the Wolf Man twice more, in Universal's 1945 *House of Dracula* and 1948 *Abbott and Costello Meet Frankenstein*), while Atwill, Zucco and Sig Rumann (as the Burgomaster of Riegelberg) all bring color, however briefly, to the film. Anne Gwynne, as Dracula's desired femme, brings a very sensual quality to her vampire-induced trance, and Elena Verdugo, with great spirit, zest and emotion, gives one of the most memorable performances of the *Frankenstein* series as the doomed Ilonka.

A special laurel must be awarded John Carradine for his lascivious Count Dracula. With his suavely cocked top hat, continental charm and sepulchrally seductive tones, Carradine's Dracula is an alluring incubus, with touches of the romantic and lustful which would later flourish in Universal's 1979 *Dracula* with Frank Langella. (Carradine would reprise the Count in Universal's 1945 *House of Dracula*.) However, the film's top performance is J. Carrol Naish's pathetic Daniel. When, heartsick over Miss Verdugo, Naish cries at the Monster, "She hates me because I'm an ugly hunchback! If it wasn't for you I'd have Talbot's body!" and begin whipping the creature with a strap, the superb actor brings true pathos and a juicy slice of Freud to the hokum.

Glenn Strange went on to play the Monster in *House of Dracula*, *Abbott and Costello Meet Frankenstein*, several tele-

Karloff, and Strange as Sam the Bartender

vision appearances, and even a 1963 amateur film, *The Adventures of the Spirit* directed by Donald Glut. During television's early days, he played another infamous heavy - Butch Cavendish, the desperado whose gang slaughtered all but one of a platoon of Texas Rangers - the one survivor becoming THE LONE RANGER. In the late 1950s, Strange took time out from his movie and television work to don a black mask and clown suit and perch atop the 150-foot mast of Hollywood's KTLA, defying the public to guess his identity. For ten days, from noon to midnight, Strange took this bizarre post, and the television station received 50,000 letters (80% guessing the mystery man to be Karloff, 15% guessing him to be Chaney!). Strange clearly held an affection for the Monster, and always gave the lion's share of credit for his fame in the role to Boris Karloff. "The Lord's been good to me," the actor said late in his life. "I've been lucky to have worked with so many grand people in this business." Glenn Strange spent the last 11 years of his life playing Sam the bartender on *Gunsmoke*; he died September 20, 1973, at the age of 74.

The profits from *House of Frankenstein* abetted Universal in achieving a fiscal 1945 profit of $4 million. Yet the battle for horror supremacy went on. Ten days after *House of Frankenstein* completed shooting, Universal faced true horror when Boris Karloff, free of his Universal contract, signed with Val Lewton's outfit at RKO, where he so chillingly portrayed *The Body Snatcher* (1945), directed by Robert Wise and featuring Bela Lugosi. Not long before his death in 1969, Karloff, in his gentle, diplomatic style, stated his feelings on Glenn Strange's Monster:

Well, he wasn't as lucky as I was. I got the cream of it, being the first. I know I wished him lots of luck...hoping it would do as much for him as it did for me, but....

Opening day at New York City's Rialto Theater

HOUSE OF FRANKENSTEIN

PRODUCER: Paul Malvern
EXECUTIVE PRODUCER: Joseph Gershenson
DIRECTOR: Erle C. Kenton
ORIGINAL STORY: Curt Siodmak
SCREENPLAY: Edward T. Lowe
PHOTOGRAPHY: George Robinson
ART DIRECTION: John B. Goodman & Martin Obzina
MUSICAL SCORE & DIRECTION: Hans J. Salter
SOUND DIRECTOR: Bernard B. Brown
SOUND TECHNICIAN: William Hedgcock
SET DECORATIONS: Russell A. Gausman
                       & A.J. Gilmore
FILM EDITOR: Philip Cahn
GOWNS: Vera West
ASSISTANT DIRECTORS: William Tummel
                       & Phil Bowles
SPECIAL PHOTOGRAPHY: John P. Fulton
SPECIAL EFFECTS MAN: Carl Elmendorf
MAKEUP: Jack P. Pierce & Otto Lederer
CAMERA OPERATOR: Eddie Cohen
ASSISTANT CAMERAMAN: Walter Bluemel
HAIR DRESSER: Carla Hadley
WARDROBE: Leroy Hommedieu
MICROPHONE: Clark Woodruff
PROP MAN: Eddie Keys
GRIP: Roland Smith
STILL MAN: Sherman Clark & Don Keyes
SCRIPT CLERK: Connie Earle
GAFFER: Max Nippell

Filmed under the shooting title THE DEVIL'S BROOD at Universal City and Sherwood Forest, California from 4 April 1944 - 8 May, 1944; opened at the Rialto Theatre, New York City, December 15, 1944.

THE PLAYERS

Dr. Gustav Niemann .... Boris Karloff
Larry Talbot .... Lon Chaney
Count Dracula .... John Carradine
Rita Hussman .... Anne Gwynne
Carl Hussman .... Peter Coe
Inspector Arnz .... Lionel Atwill
Professor Bruno Lampini .... George Zucco
Ilonka .... Elena Verdugo
            and
Daniel .... J. Carrol Naish
            with
Burgomaster Hussman .... Sig Rumann
Fejos .... William Edmunds
Toberman .... Charles Miller
Muller .... Philip Van Zandt
Hertz .... Julius Tannen
Meier .... Hans Herbert
Born .... Dick Dickinson
Gerlach .... George Lynn
Strauss .... Michael Mark
Hoffman .... Olaf Hytten
Ullman .... Frank Reicher
Dr. Geissler .... Brandon Hurst
The Monster .... Glenn Strange
Urla .... Belle Mitchell
Driver .... Eddie Cobb
Prison Guard .... Charles Wagenheim
Villager .... Joe Kirk
Double for Karloff .... Carey Loftin
Double for Naish .... Billy Jones
Double for Atwill .... George Plues

Boris Karloff

John Carradine

Lon Chaney

Anne Gwynne

Peter Coe

Glenn Strange

Lionel Atwill

J. Caroll Naish

Hans J. Salter

Jack P. Pierce

Curt Siodmak

Behind the Scenes

J. Carrol Naish, Glenn Strange, Lon Chaney Jr. and Boris Karloff celebrate Elena Verdugo's birthday during the shooting.

Ole Olsen and Glenn Strange share a common love for Batman Comics.

John Carradine's evening stagework catches up with him while shooting at Universal during the day.

Anne Gwynne and Carradine. The original caption for this photo is: HE'S A LADY KILLER - AND HOW!

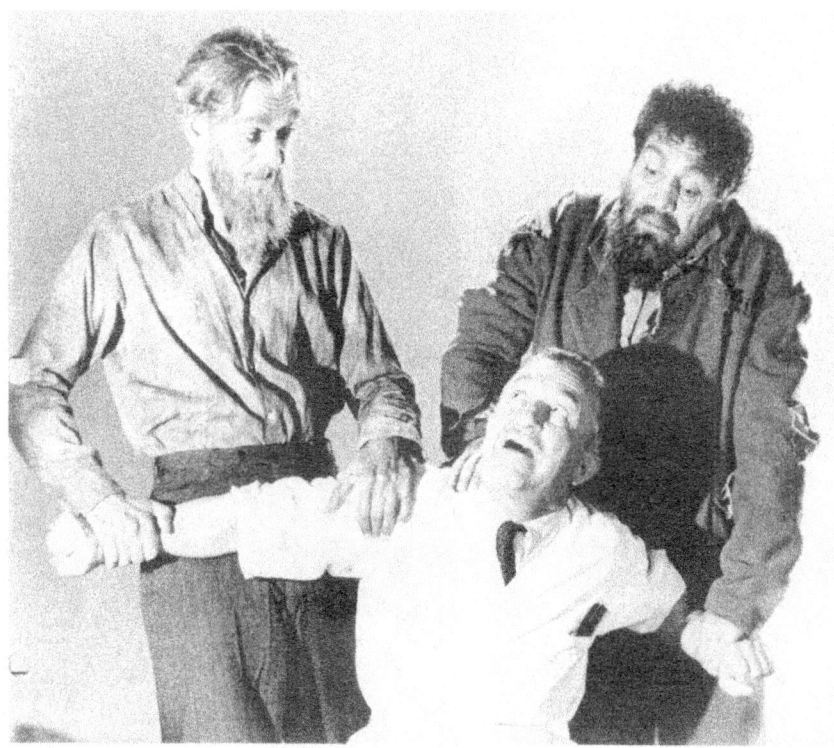

Boris Karloff and J. Carrol Naish get revenge on makeup artist Jack Pierce while shooting the prison sequence in the opening of the film.

Chaney, even in full body makeup, would take time to pose with friends.

Elena Verdugo giving the Wolf Man a pedicure.

J. Carrol Naish's daughter, Elaine, brought in her godmother's jewels for Elena Verdugo to wear. Elaine's godmother was Leslie Carter, a popular stage actress of the time.

J. Carrol Naish with his daughter and friend

Sig Rumann hamming it up for a publicity shot

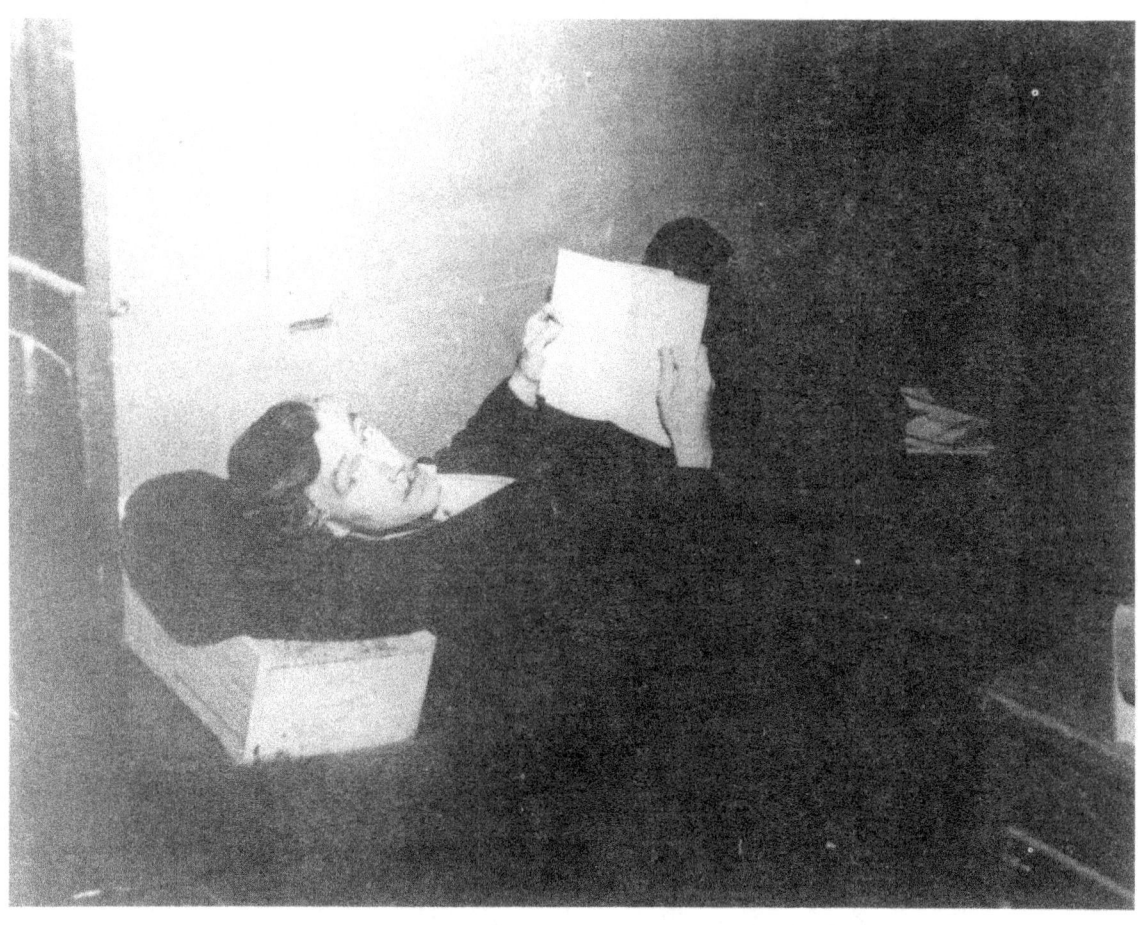
Carradine caught off guard again while studying his Shakespeare during breaks.

Boris Karloff, Director Earle C. Kenton, Lon Chaney Jr. and Producer Paul Malvern present to Elena Verdugo a book of Fairy Tales as a birthday present.

The powers-that-be at Universal during the late 1930's and 1940's: (Left) William Scully, Nate Blumberg, President and Vice President Clifford Work (Right) Production Executive William Goetz and Leo Spitz with actor Danny Kaye (Courtesy Bison Archives).

Peter Coe and Anne Gwynne pose for a series of shots where the crew and cast hide Peter's car to keep him on the lot. He had just enlisted in the Marines and was leaving a few days after the completion of HOUSE OF FRANKENSTEIN.

Music

Hans J. Salter's own score for the sequence where Karloff brings Carradine, as Count Dracula, back to life.
(Copyright 1944 Universal Music Corporation)

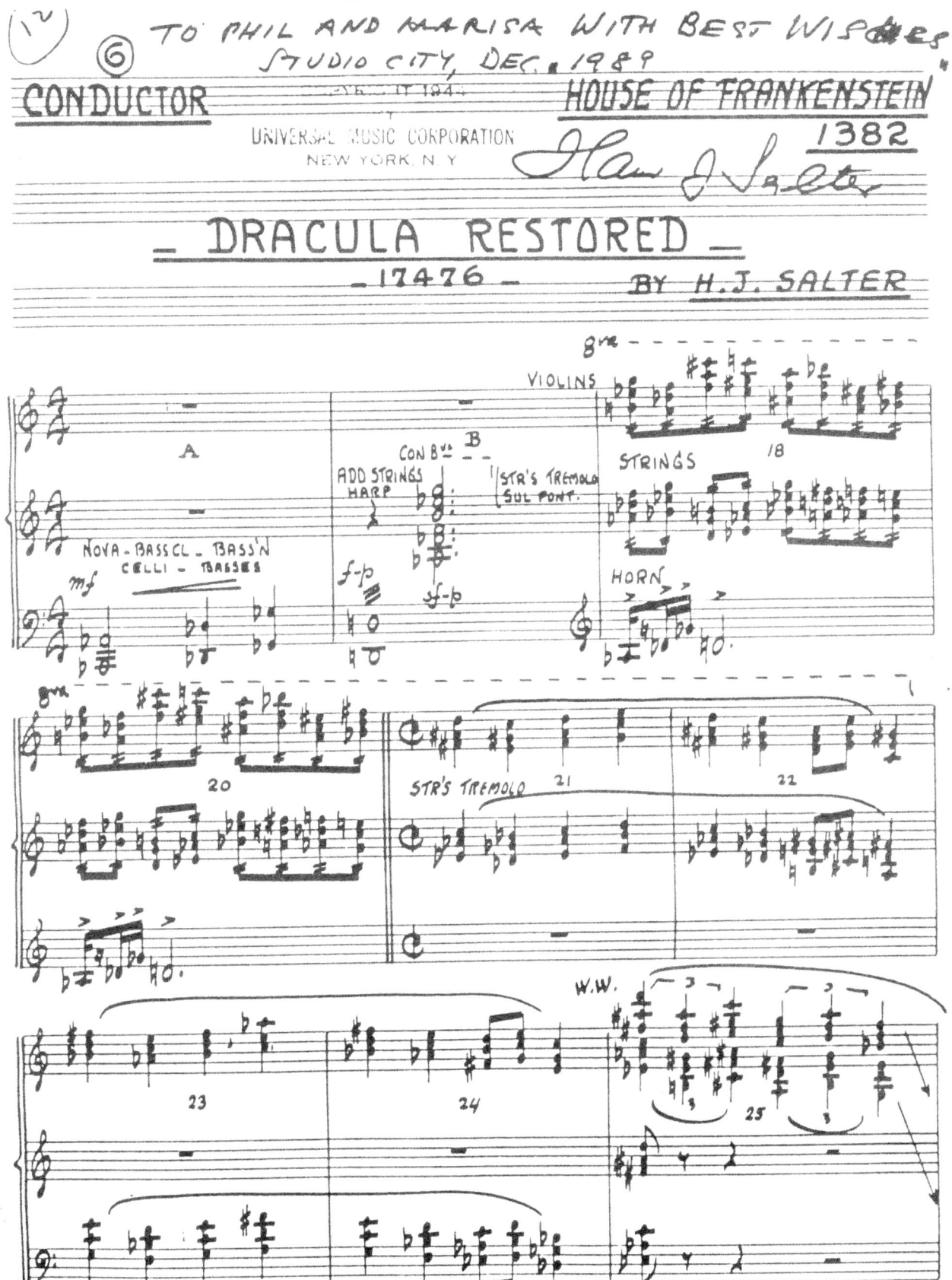

Salter's score showng the main theme and cover sheets for various sequences - Frank Skinner, Co-Composer

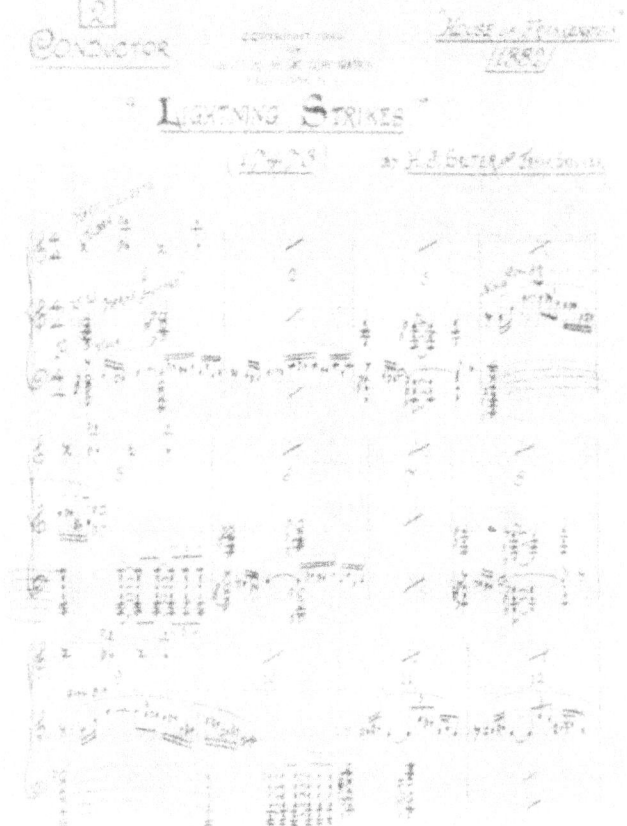

Exterior sets

(Above) George Robinson, Cinematographer, sets up an outdoor shot while Karloff and Naish kill time. (Below) the scene in the final film.

(Above) These sets still exist and can be seen on the Universal Tour, Universal City Hollywood.
(Below) Maria Montez visits the set with her three sisters to watch the shooting on the old HUNCHBACK OF NOTRE DAME (1923) exteriors. The arched stairwell directly behind her was used for the climax of the film as the Monster attempts to escape with Karloff. These sets, also known as the European Village, were destroyed by fire around 1975.

Stunt doubles for Karloff and Naish flee from the police after Dracula kidnaps Anne Gwynne - Shot on the Corrigan Ranch - Hopeville, Simi Valley. (Below) a different angle of the escape road on the same property.

UNIVERSAL PICTURES COMPANY, INC.
PACIFIC COAST STUDIOS

ASSISTANT DIRECTOR'S DAILY REPORT

Date MONDAY, April 24th,

Director ERLE C. KENTON Title THE DEVIL'S BROOD Picture No. 1382 Producer P.

Starting Date 4/4/44 Finishing Date 5/8/44 Schedule Days 30 Days W.

Company Call	1:00 PM	Total Pages in Script	125	Schedule Status
Time Started	2:20 PM	Taken Today	4	
Time Finished	3:00 AM	Taken Previously	72 ½	
Time Dismissed	3:00 AM	Total To Date	76 ½	
Camera Set-ups	18 (2 cameras)	To Do	48 ¾	
Meal Hours	2 hrs	Must Average Per Day	4 ½	

Where Worked EXT. LAMPINI'S WAGON (Process Stage) INT. HALL (Stage 17)
Reasons for Delays EXT. ROAD & MARSH (Nagana Rocks)

Minutes		Numbers of Script Scenes Shot Today
Total Today	3'40"	181 – 160 – ~~162~~ – 371 – 373 – 392 – 398 – 441 – 4
Previously Reported	57'10"	444 – 445 – 446 – 447 – 448 – 449 – 450 – ~~451~~ –
Total to Date	60'50"	~~454~~ – ~~455~~

STILLS		Total Scenes In Script	Total Shot Today	Total Shot To Date	Total Remaining To Do
Today	To Date	455	21	260	
10	87	Exterior Weather Conditions			

Cast and Day Players		Time Called A.M.	Time Called P.M.	Time Dismissed A.M.	Time Dismissed P.M.	Meal Hours Out	STAFF
BORIS KARLOFF			1:00	3:00	–	2	(As of 4/14/44)
J. CARROL NAISH			1:00		5:35	--	
ELENA VERDUGO	(C)		4:00		5:15	--	Plus extra Camera crew –
LON CHANEY			4:00		5:30	--	OPERATOR: Perry Finnerm
GLEN STRANGE *	(C)		7:30	3		1	ASST. CAM. John Silver
CHARLES MILLER			7:30	3		1	" " Mike Walsh
JULIUS TANNEN	(C)		7:30	3		1	
DICK DICKINSON	(C)		7:30	3		1	
HANS HERBERT	(C)		7:30	3		1	
JOE KIRK	(C)		7:30	3		1	
DOUBLE							
CAREY LOFTIN (Karloff)			7:00	3		1	
* STRANGE in Make-up			3:00 PM				Extras and Miscellaneous
							4 Stand-ins at $ 8.

A sample of Assistant Directors William Tummel and Phil Bowles' Daily Production Reports. Note the name of Karloff's double and the cameraman and his assistant. Also, the location name "Nagana Rocks" is from an earlier popular Universal film.

Scenes from *House of Frankenstein*

Mad Doctor Gustav Niemann (Karloff) escapes from prison

Burgomaster Hussman, Inspector Arnz and Carl Hussman are coerced into seeing Professor Lampini's Chamber of Horrors show

After killing the real Professor Lampini and his assistant, Dr. Niemann and Daniel take their place in order to seek revenge on the men who sent them to prison. Daniel nervously watches Inspector Arnz as Carl pays the admission fee to see the actual skeleton of Count Dracula.

Count Dracula is revived when Dr. Niemann removes the stake from his heart.

Count Dracula seduces Rita Hussman

After escaping the police of Regelberg, Niemann and Daniel come upon a Gypsy camp and save Ilonka from a cruel beating.

Ilonka leaves with the mad doctor and hunchback.

Dr. Niemann's discovery while searching for Dr. Frankenstein's records.

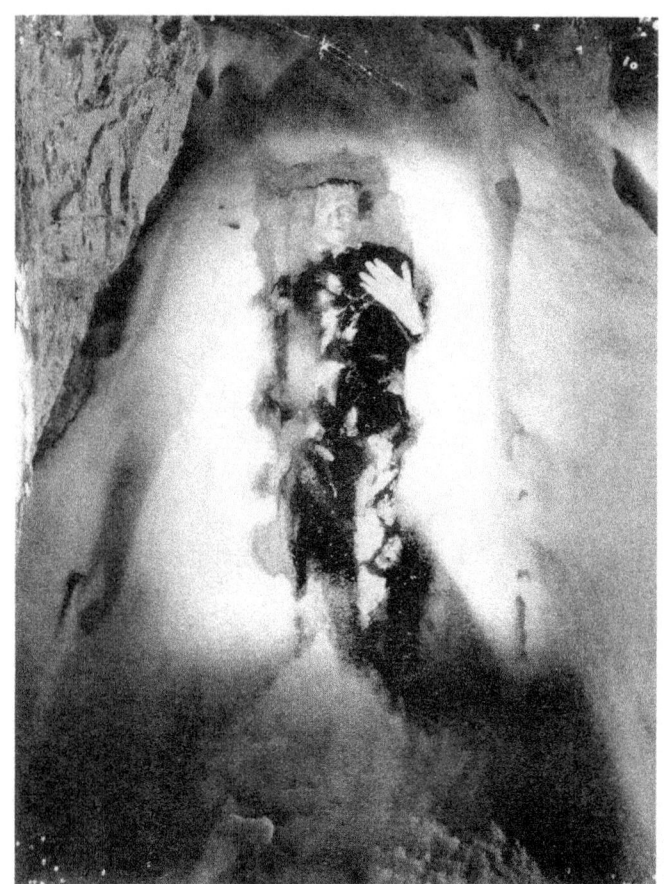
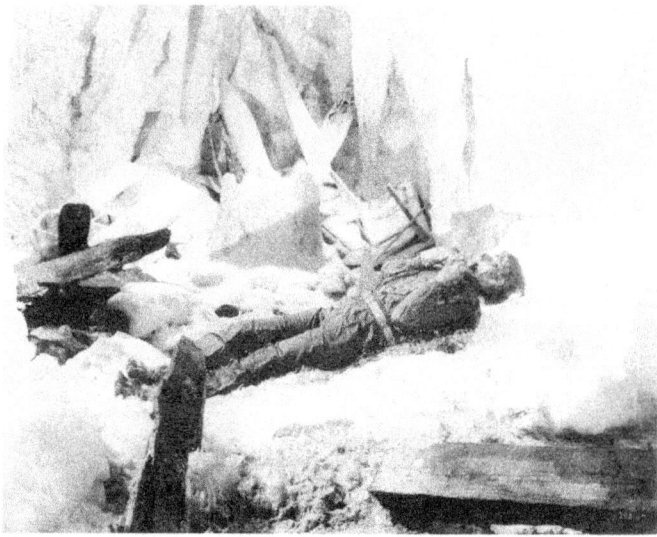

The Frankenstein Monster and the Wolf Man are found frozen in the ice caverns where the flood at the end of FRANKENSTEIN MEETS THE WOLF MAN deposited them.

A revived Larry Talbot gives the Doctor the Frankenstein Records.

The Devil's Brood travel to the mad doctor's laboratory to revive the Monster and cure the Wolf Man.

 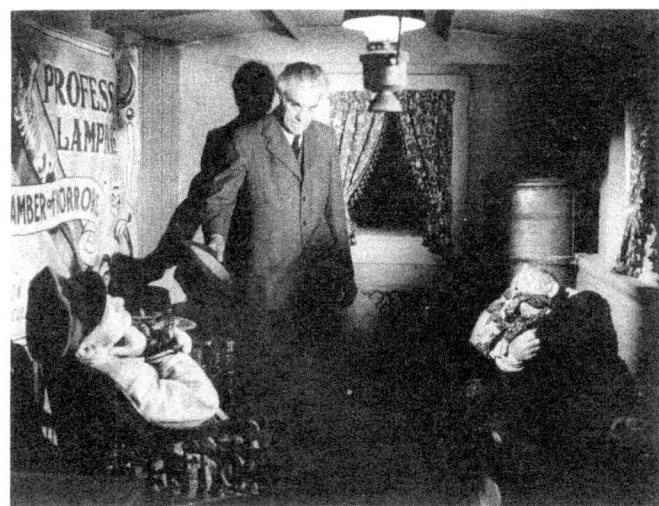

Dr. Niemann begins his revenge on the men who sent him to prison.

Ilonka and Larry fall in love.

The revival of the Monster begins.

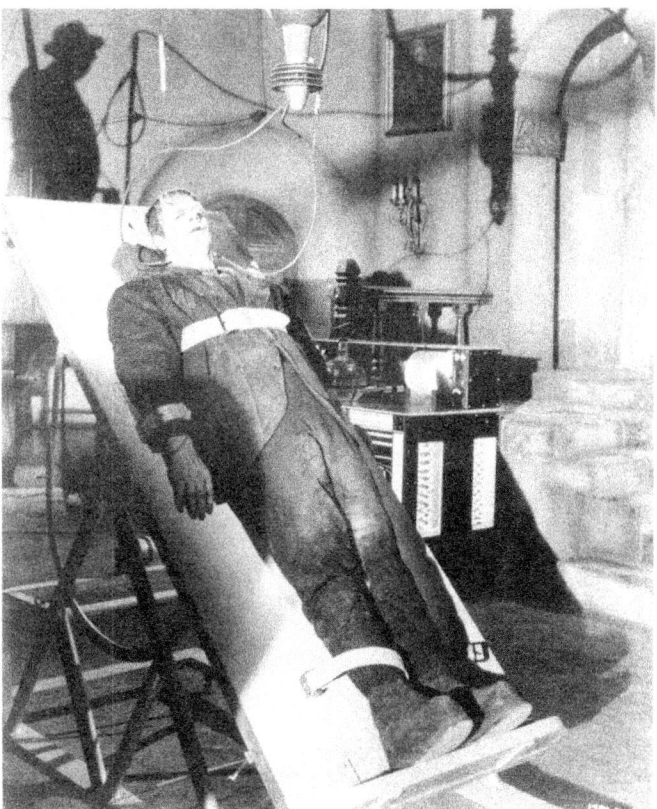

Director Kenton's shadow accidentally appears in this scene (behind the Monster to the top left).

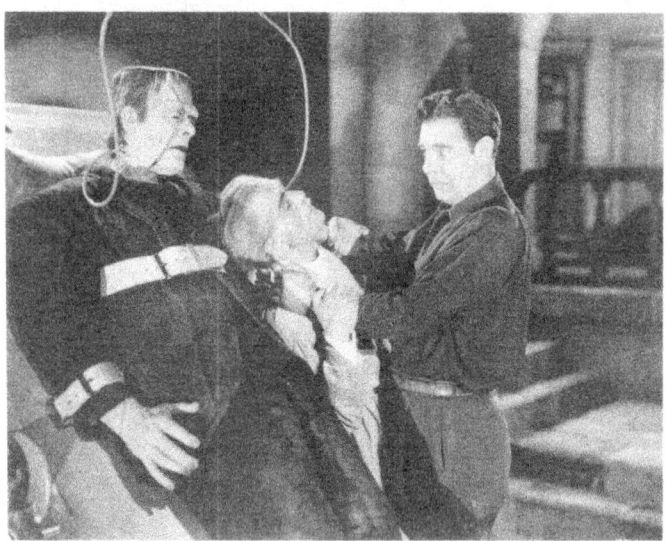

Talbot grows impatient (tonight there will be a full moon), but he stops when the Doctor warns that without his surgical skills Talbot is doomed as the Wolf Man.

The cure comes too late and Ilonka is killed by the Wolf Man, but not before she shoots him with a silver bullet.

The Mob reaches the castle and finds that the Monster is escaping.

*The Monster sinks in the quicksand while trying to save Dr. Niemann.
(The following year, the Monster would rise again in HOUSE OF DRACULA.)*

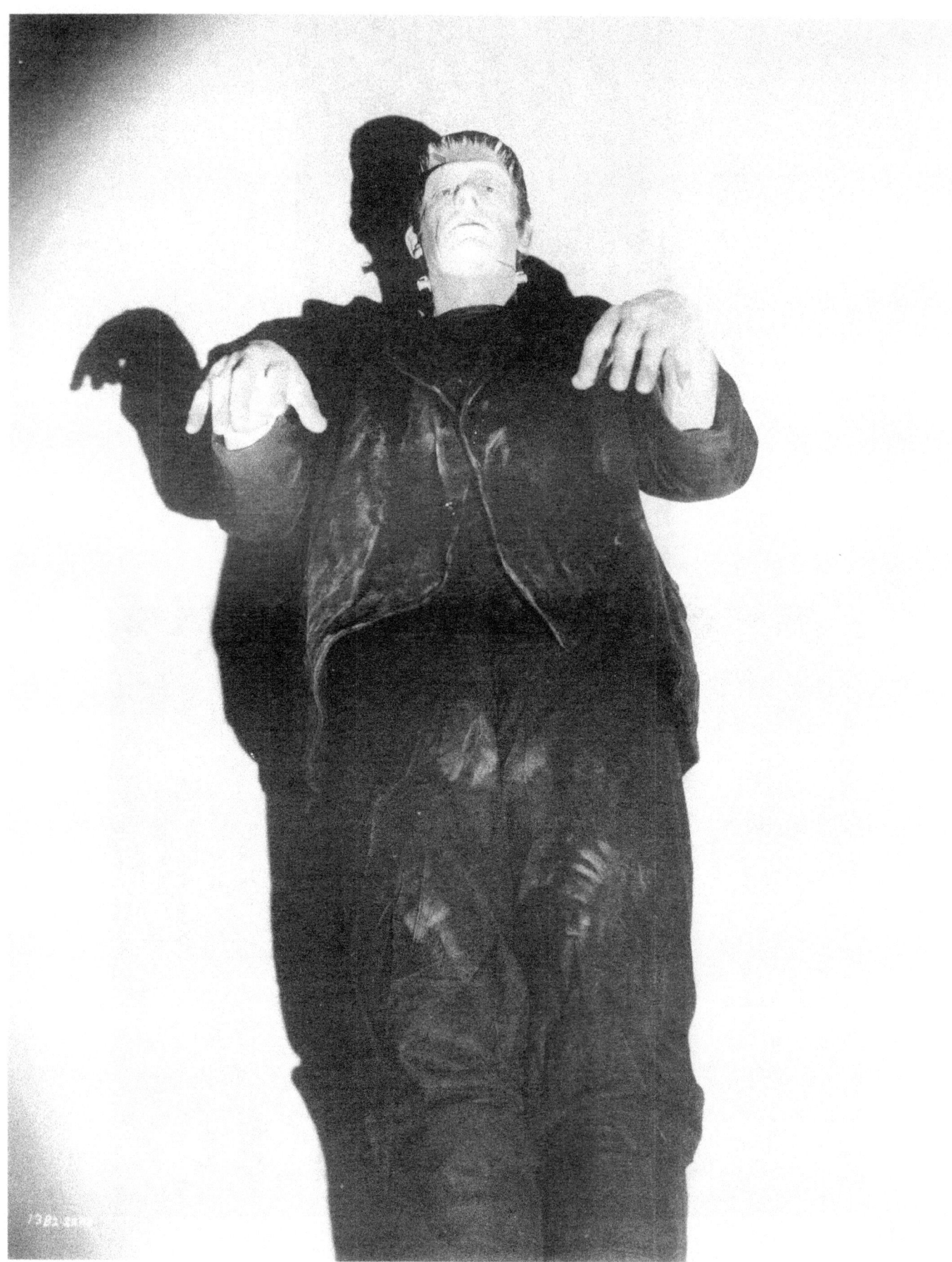

House of ~~Frankenstein~~
~~DESTINY~~

Based on Characters Created by

Bram Stoker
Mrs. Percy B. Shelley
Curtis Siodmak

SCREENPLAY BY

Edward T. Lowe

From an Idea by

Curtis Siodmak

Rare example of Publicity Department paste-up before title was changed to HOUSE OF FRANKENSTEIN.

"DESTINY"

FADE IN

1   EXT. COUNTRYSIDE - LONG SHOT - <u>NIGHT</u>

It is a stormy, rain-drenched night. Moving slowly up the slope of a rutty, muddy road is a caravan of two vehicles, drawn by four laboring horses.

The first of the vehicles is a large, traveling-show van. On the high seat of it is the driver, huddled into a capacious, glistening oil-skin coat.

The second unit of the caravan is a commodious living-wagon, its curtained windows illuminated by a light burning inside.

Following a flash of lightning which etches the scene into harsh brilliance, the MAIN TITLE DISSOLVES IN.

                    DESTINY

The various CREDIT TITLES play against the caravan's slow progress, so that when the last title DISSOLVES OUT, the CAMERA, WHICH HAS BEEN MOVING TOWARD the outfit, is now close enough to reveal lettering on the side of the big van, illuminated by another flash of lightning.

            PROFESSOR LAMPINI'S
            CHAMBER OF HORRORS

As the caravan labors up the slope and as the living-wagon passes through, the CAMERA CONTINUES ITS ONWARD MOVEMENT toward a tall, stone, spiked wall into which are set massive iron gates.

Beyond the wall on an eminence is a stone-built structure of medieval architecture, its turrets and battlements gaunt against the storm-torn night.

As the CAMERA MOVES CLOSER TO THE GATES, one of its stone supports is brought CLOSER AND CLOSER until letters carved into one of the blocks, are revealed in a flash of lightning.

                NEUSTADT PRISON

As the CAMERA MOVES TOWARD THIS RAIN-DRENCHED LEGEND,

                                        DISSOLVE TO

2. INT. PRISON CORRIDOR - GRILL AND DOOR - CLOSE SHOT

The iron bars of this 10" x 10" hinged grill opening cut into the heavy woodwork of the ancient door, are just close enough together to prevent a straining, talon-like hand from unfastening the rusty iron hasp which holds the grill shut. The owner of this hand is not revealed at the moment in the fitful offscene light --but as he withdraws his arm and the fingers of both his hands grasp the grill and rattle it violently, we hear the wrathful voice of:

> DR. NIEMANN
> Bring me the chalk you promised me!
> This is the day you give me my chalk!

During this the CAMERA ANGLES AWAY from the grill, to reveal a basement corridor in the prison.

Up high in the stone work of its vaulted construction is a barred window through which lightning flashes illuminate the scene at intervals. Opposite this wall, revealed as the CAMERA PULLS BACK into a MEDIUM FULL SHOT, is the door of the dungeon-like cell we have just left -- and also another similar door, a little distance from it.

Aside from the flashes of lightning, the only other illumination is from a wick, burning in an open stone receptacle which is integral with the stonework of the wall.

The upscene end of the corridor is separated from another which intersects it, by iron bars into which is set a door of similar construction. This door is being unlocked by a not too pleasant guard, the light from whose lantern - at the moment standing upon the floor - dispels a little part of the gloom and makes the sweating walls glisten eerily. Beside the lantern is a chunk of coarse bread and an earthenware pitcher, containing water.

> DR. NIEMANN'S VOICE
> Do you hear me, you fools? I want my
> chalk! Give me my chalk!

The guard picks up the lantern, bread and pitcher and clumps his way downscene over the flagstones toward the door of Niemann's cell.

> GUARD
> Be quiet in there!

Niemann's face is now seen as the guard hangs his lantern on a bracket and starts to unfasten the grill.

Niemann, actually a man of about forty-five, appears much older because of his beard and unkempt hair.

CONTINUED

2   CONTINUED

NIEMANN
Give me my chalk! I must get
on with my work!

GUARD
(pushing water pitcher
through the grill)
Take this.

Niemann slaps the pitcher from the guard's hand and sends it crashing to the floor.

NIEMANN
I want chalk! Chalk!

He thrusts his arm suddenly through the opening, closes it about the man's neck in a scissors lock and pulls his head forward against the door.

NIEMANN
Now will you give it to me?

GUARD
(unintelligibly)
Let me go! Help! Help!

He drops the bread and tries to tear Niemann's arm from around his throat. Failing in this, he frantically reaches into a pocket of his coat and takes out a handful of square pieces of chalk, which he thrusts through the opening.

3   INT. NIEMANN'S CELL - AT DOOR - CLOSE SHOT

Niemann, a tall, bony caricature of what was once a handsome man, releases his lock on the guard's neck and sinks to his knees, gathering the pieces frantically in his bony hands.

NIEMANN
My chalk! Now I can go on with
my work!

4   INT. PRISON CORRIDOR - NEAR NIEMANN'S DOOR - MED. CLOSE SHOT

The infuriated guard picks up the bread, hurls it through the opening and slams the grill, locking it.

GUARD
Try that again and I'll put you
in solitary confinement, you
half-baked Frankenstein!

5   INT. NIEMANN'S CELL - AT DOOR - MED. CLOSE SHOT

Niemann, getting to his feet, puts his face close to the door and screams his rage at the guard.

> NIEMANN
> Don't profane his name with your dirty lips! Frankenstein was a genius in whose footsteps I shall follow, when I get out of here.

6   INT. PRISON CORRIDOR - NEAR NIEMANN'S DOOR - MED. CLOSE

The furious guard is loosening the neck band of his shirt to fill his empty lungs.

> GUARD
> Trying to imitate Frankenstein brought you here, you jibbering crackpot! If I had anything to say about it, you'd never get out!

Niemann presses his distorted face closer to the grill.

> NIEMANN
> But I will! And when I do, I will open your skull and give you the brain of a toad!

A flash of lightning illuminates Niemann's face, etching it into a cameo of rage and hatred. The guard draws away from the door, snarling.

> GUARD
> Ar-r-r-h...

He spits his disgust through the grill and starts out.

7   INT. NIEMANN'S CELL - AT DOOR - MED. CLOSE SHOT

As Niemann moves away from the door the CAMERA PANS, disclosing a flagstoned dungeon of rather large size and irregular shape whose sweating walls glisten in the light which filters through the grill and also through a barred opening, high up in the wall above it. There is a stone shelf on which is a disintegrating straw mattress, serving as a bed. The room is otherwise bare.

On the wall, revealed eerily by the lightning flashes are chalk-drawn chemical formulas and diagrams of surgical instruments and complicated high-frequency electrical apparatus.

CONTINUED

7   CONTINUED

As Niemann crosses the room, the CHANGING ANGLE shows a barred, arched opening through which may be seen the interior of a similar, but smaller cell, adjoining.

Standing with his hands clutching two of the rusty bars is a hulking figure, a hunchback whose eyes, catlike and unblinking, follow Niemann's every move. This hunchback's name is DANIEL.

The CHANGING ANGLE now loses Daniel and follows Niemann's approach to a large, unbroken expanse of wall upon which is a chalk-drawn presentation of Niemann's laboratory, to be seen later.

The CAMERA MOVES with Niemann as he draws closer to "his work", the CLOSER VIEW emphasizing two surgical operating tables, on one of which lies the covered figure of a man. On the second, also covered by a sheet, is the body of a giant dog.

Electrical apparatus of strange concepts stand near the tables. Wires, leading from this apparatus, are connected to a complex board of meters and switches from which other pairs of wires branch out and connect with terminal pads, fastened by means of metal bands to the heads of the man and the dog.

Now near the table on which lies the dog, Niemann uses a block of chalk, to shade in the convolutions on a large, human brain, drawn above the dog's table.

                NIEMANN
           (glancing off, toward
            the hunchback)
To resume, friend Daniel...

8   CLOSER SHOT - NIEMANN AND DRAWING

Extending from various "lobes" of the brain are a number of lines, marked "A", "B", "C", etc. As he talks, Niemann draws a circle around the brain and extends a line from it, pointing the end into an arrow, which touches the dog's skull.

                NIEMANN (continues)
This brain, taken from the man and
transplanted into the skull of the
dog, would have given _him_ the mind
of a human being....

Pausing a moment, Niemann draws a line across the point where the spinal cord enters the brain:

                        CONTINUED

8   CONTINUED

> NIEMANN (continued)
> Frankenstein would have severed the
> spinal cord at that point...But I
> am not quite certain he was right --
> not quite certain...

As he studies the drawing, the CAMERA ANGLES AWAY from
him and goes toward Daniel, standing in the same position as first seen, his never blinking eyes fixed on
Niemann, offscene. When he speaks, it is in a purring,
insinuating voice.

> DANIEL
> Could Frankenstein have made me
> like other men...?

9   MED. CLOSE SHOT - NIEMANN - NEAR WALL

> NIEMANN
> (fanatically)
> Frankenstein and the heavens' lightnings
> gave life to a body which he built from
> parts of other bodies, which had died...

The CAMERA MOVES with Niemann, following him to the arch
where he and Daniel talk to each other through the bars.

> NIEMANN (continued)
> Yes, Daniel -- he could have made you
> like other men...

The hunchback's eyes glow. His fingers tighten around
the iron bars as he tenses forward.

> DANIEL
> Did you know -- Dr. Frankenstein...?

> NIEMANN
> (sadly regretful)
> My brother, who assisted him in his
> early work, learned a few of his
> secrets. He passed them on to me,
> when he died...

> DANIEL
> Then -- you could give me -- another
> body...?

> NIEMANN
> (frowning)
> Had I but Frankenstein's records to
> guide me, I could duplicate his work --

CONTINUED

9   CONTINUED

The CAMERA PULLS BACK into a MEDIUM SHOT, in which Niemann walks to and fro across the room.

> NIEMANN
> (continues)
> -- and go even farther...
> (tapping his forehead)
> In here, is the concept of a new technique --

10 CLOSE SHOT - NIEMANN

His eyes glow with a fanatical light as he continues:

> NIEMANN
> -- complete except for the missing procedures of Frankenstein's final experiments -- which I will seek, when I leave this place...

The CAMERA PANS HIM until Daniel comes into view. The hunchback's unblinking eyes are riveted on Niemann's face.

> NIEMANN
> (continued)
> With those, I could give you not only a perfect body, but a new mind -- a brain built from parts of a dozen others, and perfect brains!

11 EXT. PRISON - FULL SHOT - (MINIATURE) - NIGHT

As though in anger, the heavens are split by a jagged fork of lightning.

12 INT. NIEMANN'S CELL - MEDIUM CLOSE AT ARCH

Lost in his dreams, Niemann's gaze is fixed in space.

> NIEMANN
> My work that night, drew aside the veil --

As Niemann moves away from the arch, the CAMERA ANGLES SO THAT the picture of the laboratory becomes the background.

> NIEMANN
> (continued)
> -- and gave me a glimpse of the miracles the future might hold...

13   CLOSE SHOT - NIEMANN

As he stands looking at the picture, Niemann's voice becomes harsh and bitter.

              NIEMANN
              (continues)
...But I was interrupted...Before
I could complete my experiments,
the door of my laboratory was broken
open by a mob of howling villagers...
            (his eyes burn
              with resentment)
They threatened my life -- because,
like Frankenstein...

The CAMERA PANS WITH HIM as he walks back to the arch.

              NIEMANN
              (continued)
...I also took bodies of the newly
dead from their graves to carry on
my work...
            (speaking directly
              to the hunchback)
Of what use to anyone but a scientist is a body that is dead...?
            (Daniel shakes his
              head inarticulately)
Of *no* use, my friend...
            (Niemann's face
              hardens)
But they didn't see it that way.
After the trial, they sent me here --

14   CLOSE SHOT - NIEMANN
              NIEMANN
              (continued)
-- and here I have remained for fifteen years, forgotten.
            (his eyes narrow)
But *I* haven't forgotten!
            (he counts the names
              off on his fingers)
There is Strauss - who told that he
saw me in the graveyard, that night...
            (another finger)
Ullman, who assisted me -- then testified for the State, in order to save
his own miserable hide...
            (with particular hatred)
And Ludwig Hussman, the Burgomaster --
who said the village prison was too
good for me - and who had me sent here,
to die - and rot...

vk

15   CLOSE SHOT - NIEMANN AND DANIEL

Niemann's gaze shifts to the hunchback's face as he comes out of his retrospections.

> NIEMANN
> No, friend Daniel...I haven't forgotten --
> as they who called me a madman will have
> reason to know, when I get out of here...

> DANIEL
> (an almost inaudible purr)
> But you aren't mad - are you, Dr. Niemann...?

> NIEMANN
> It is they who are crazy! The secrets
> of life and death are mine, shared only
> by the heavens which gave us being...

16   EXT. PRISON - FULL SHOT - (MINIATURE)

As if to wreak wrathful vengeance against the man who dares to dream of usurping God's work, a flash of lightning slashes the clouds and hurls its blasting force through a window of the ancient building.

17   INT. PRISON - GUARDS' ROOM - FULL SHOT - NIGHT

The guard previously seen, and a burly companion are engaged in rolling dice from a cup as the blast disintegrates the window and, accompanied by ominous crackling sounds, forms itself into a ball of irradiant brilliance which illuminates the room with a weird, unearthly glow.

> FIRST GUARD
> Ball lightning!!!

He and his companion overturn the table and chairs as they run from the room in panic-stricken terror.

The ball of destruction, from which "trees" of brush electricity crackle into the air, seems to hesitate uncertainly. Then, sucked along by the draft, it floats into the corridor, upscene, as a terrific thunder clasp reverberates and echoes against the bare stone walls.

18   INT. NIEMANN'S CELL - AT ARCH - MED. CLOSE SHOT

The echoing thunder shakes the very foundations on which the prison stands. As the bars rattle in their sockets and little sprays of static electricity run up and down between them, Daniel raises his unblinking eyes heavenward in quaking fear.

19 INT. PRISON - CORRIDOR TO GUARDS' ROOM - FULL SHOT

   As the ball of lightning floats in the air over the flagstones TOWARD THE CAMERA, sparks leap from its surface
   and sizzle against the walls on either side.

20 INT. PRISON - CORRIDOR OF NIEMANN'S CELL - FULL SHOT

   The radiant ball of energy floats into view in the intersecting corridor and, in its passage to the corridor of
   Niemann's and Daniel's cells, sears the separating iron
   bars into incandescent brilliance, leaving a round opening
   in the iron work as it passes through and floats lightly
   along.

21 INT. NIEMANN'S CELL - MED. SHOT

   Niemann moves swiftly to the door. As he peers into the
   corridor, his face is illuminated by the blinding brillianc
   from the ball.

22 INT. PRISON - CORRIDOR OF NIEMANN'S CELL - REVERSE SHOT

   The ball of destructive force is floating in the corridor
   near the cell door...

23 INT. PRISON - NIEMANN'S CELL - NEAR DOOR - CLOSE SHOT

   As Niemann sees what is about to happen, he turns from
   the door and runs quickly toward the arch...As he throws
   himself to the floor, Daniel, terror stricken, follows
   his example....

24 INT. PRISON - CORRIDOR OF NIEMANN'S CELL

   The ball of lightning sinks downward. As it hits the
   floor, it explodes with a mighty roar.

25 INT. PRISON - NIEMANN'S CELL - FULL SHOT - TOWARD DOOR

   A portion of the corridor wall, together with a part of
   the wall which separates Niemann's cell from Daniel's,
   is crumpling into the room.

                         NIEMANN
                   (springing to his feet)
              Come, my friend! We are free!

                                                    CONTINUED

25   CONTINUED

Daniel runs through the opening in the broken wall between
the cells and follows Niemann, who is already clambering
over the debris of masonry into --

26   INT. PRISON - CORRIDOR OF NIEMANN'S CELL - MED. FULL SHOT

Niemann, climbing over the debris, drags the quaking
Daniel with him along the edge of a jagged opening which
the lightning has blasted through the flag-stoned floor.

A loud, rumbling sound OFFSCENE, makes them stop. They
look toward --

27   BARRED ARCH TO INTERSECTING CORRIDOR - MED. SHOT

The ceiling in the guards' corridor beyond the opening,
is crumbling downward. The masonry above the arched
opening gives way, bending the iron bars like they were
made of rubber.

28   NEAR EDGE OF OPENING IN FLOOR - MED. CLOSE SHOT

Niemann, seeing that he and Daniel are trapped, looks
down into the yawning pit in the floor.

29   DOWNWARD ANGLE INTO PIT - MED. SHOT

Eight or ten feet below the corridor floor can be seen
the curved masonry of an ancient sewer, all but closed by
the debris which has fallen into it.

30   CORRIDOR NEAR EDGE OF PIT - CLOSE SHOT

Daniel's fear-stricken gaze is following Niemann's as
another ominous rumble of falling masonry brings Niemann
to a decision. He grasps Daniel by his arm.

                    NIEMANN
          Come!

As Daniel hangs back, Niemann drags him down the debris-
strewn side of the pit into --

31   INT. SEWER - FULL SHOT

This ellipse-shaped sewer is just high enough for a man
to stand upright. A foot or so of water is flowing in
it from the storm. Niemann and Daniel, upscene in the
pit's debris of masonry and rubble, clamber over the rocks
and into the passage just as a mass of collapsing masonry
drops into the pit behind them with a deafening roar.

32 INT. SEWER - REVERSE ANGLE - FULL SHOT

In a view which excludes the pit, Niemann and Daniel are plunging through the water into the blackness of the sewer ahead of them as the scene

DISSOLVES INTO

33 EXT. RAVINE - MOUTH OF SEWER - MED. SHOT - <u>NIGHT</u>

It is raining. A flash of lightning shows Niemann and Daniel as they come from the mouth of the ancient sewer, the water from which empties into a small gully.

The CAMERA PANS with them as they plunge their way through the water and loses them in a

DISSOLVE TO

34 EXT. COUNTRYSIDE - MED. SHOT

Rain and storm effects continue as a DOWNWARD ANGLE along the sloping side of the ravine picks up Niemann and Daniel, PANNING WITH THEM as they claw their way up to level ground. Here, they stop in a MEDIUM FOREGROUND SHOT which shows Lampini's two vehicles, mired in the muddy road, beyond. A lantern is hanging on a bracket at the end of the large van - one of whose rear wheels is down to its hub in the mud.

Another flash of lightning shows a man, Lampini, putting his shoulder to the mired wheel while the driver, ahead, cracks his whip across the flanks of the straining horses.

35 NEAR ROAD - NIEMANN AND DANIEL - CLOSE SHOT

Glancing at Daniel with a crafty expression, Niemann nods in the direction of Lampini's caravan. The CAMERA PANS with them as they start toward it.

36 LAMPINI'S CARAVAN NEAR END OF LARGE VAN - MED. CLOSE SHOT

The efforts of the straining horses, coupled with Lampini's are still inadequate to unmire the wheel. Lampini, whose back is to CAMERA, doesn't see or hear the entrance of Niemann and Daniel.

CONTINUED

36 CONTINUED

> NIEMANN
> We will help you.
>
> DANIEL
> (holding out
> his arms)
> My muscles are like iron...There
> is the strength of a dozen men
> in my arms...

At the sound of the voices, LAMPINI turns. He is a man of sixty or better - a self-appointed "Professor".

> LAMPINI
> Thank you, whoever you are...
>
> NIEMANN
> Put your shoulder to the wheel
> ahead... we will handle this one.

Lampini goes toward the front part of the van. Daniel seizes one of the wheel spokes and pulls forward while Niemann, with a shoulder under a part of the wheel's rim, braces himself and strains to raise the heavy load. The driver lashes the horses' flanks with his whip and, under the combined efforts of all, the mired wheel raises out of the mud onto the more solid road.

DISSOLVE INTO

37 EXT. COUNTRYSIDE - LAMPINI'S CARAVAN - MED. LONG SHOT

The outfit is crawling along a rutty road as the scene

DISSOLVE INTO

38 INT. LAMPINI'S LIVING-WAGON - FULL SHOT - NIGHT

There is a bunk across the van's forward end, and a padded seat along one side under the curtained window. Among Lampini's luxuries, there is an old rocking-chair. The walls are covered with photographs of the show's "Horrors", along with a gaudily painted poster.

At intervals, flashes of lightning shaft through the curtained windows, accompanied by offscene rolls of thunder as the caravan jolts along through the night.

CONTINUED

38 CONTINUED

Lampini, wearing a stocking-cap and smoking a long-stemmed, meerschaum pipe, is in his rocking-chair partly facing Niemann and Daniel. They are seated on the edge of the bunk, partaking of Lampini's hospitality. Daniel is wolfing his bread and wine. Niemann, inherently a gentleman, is more fastidious in manner.

As the scene DISSOLVES IN:

> LAMPINI
> (is addressing Niemann)
> So you are a merchant who has been held for ransom by mountain bandits...?
>
> NIEMANN
> For the better part of three months....
>
> LAMPINI
> And _he_ -
> (pointing his pipestem at Daniel)
> -- is your servant...?
>
> NIEMANN
> (with a flash of hostility)
> Do you doubt me?
>
> LAMPINI
> (chuckling)
> It is a doubting world, kind sir -- as I ---

39 CLOSE SHOT - LAMPINI

He becomes unconsciously the professional showman.

> LAMPINI (cont'd)
> -- Professor Bruno Lampini, have reason to know. In my show, I have a collection of the world's most shocking horrors - but when I exhibit them, what do I get...? Doubts, jeers -- and cries of 'fake!', 'fake!'...! Ah, yes...It is a doubting world.

40 CLOSE SHOT - NIEMANN AND DANIEL

The hunchback absorbs the conversation with appropriate reactions.

Niemann, with a vague smile, looks off toward --

41   INSERT - CLOSEUP

This shows the poster previously mentioned. It proclaims:

> PROFESSOR LAMPINI'S
> Chamber of Horrors

(Upright, beneath the large letters, is a coffin in which lies a skeleton with a wooden stake driven through its chest, and beneath this is more printing.)

> Presenting the Actual Skeleton
> of
> Count Dracula
> the
> Vampire

42   CLOSE SHOT - NIEMANN

> NIEMANN
> (smiling)
> You expect your patrons to believe that the skeleton you show them --
> (he nods toward
> the poster)
> -- is really that of Count Dracula?

43   CLOSE SHOT - LAMPINI

> LAMPINI
> (lowering his voice
> to a confidential whisper)
> I, Lampini, took it -- pardon me, borrowed it -- from the cellar of Dracula's castle, in the Carpathian Mountains --

44   CLOSE SHOT - LAMPINI

> LAMPINI (cont'd)
> -- and with my own two hands, spread upon the bottom of its coffin a layer of dirt from his birthplace, so that -- by proxy, shall we say? - the skeleton of his earthbound spirit might lie at peace within its grave...

45   GROUP SHOT

Daniel, awed, shrinks closer to Niemann.

CONTINUED

45   CONTINUED

> NIEMANN
> (picking up Lampini's line)
> Until withdrawal of the wooden stake
> through his heart would set Dracula
> free again, to satisfy his unholy
> appetite for blood...?
>
> LAMPINI
> Aye...At night the giant bat would
> seek its victims.
>
> NIEMANN
> (after a second)
> Tell me, my friend -- did you
> ever exhibit your show in the
> village of Visaria...?
>
> LAMPINI
> (snorting his disgust)
> Visaria? There's a town that
> doesn't care for horrors...They
> had one of their own, some fifteen
> years ago -- when a Dr. Niemann
> tried to give a dog the mind of
> a human being...
> (angrily)
> Mayor Hussman ran me out of the place.

46   CLOSE SHOT - NIEMANN AND DANIEL

The hunchback's eyes shift to Niemann, who tenses forward.

> NIEMANN
> Is old Hussman still alive?

47   GROUP SHOT

> LAMPINI
> You know the Burgomaster....?

Niemann's eyes seem to be gazing into the past. He nods.

> NIEMANN
> I haven't seen him -- for many years.
> (his voice becomes harsh)
> But I intend -- to see him.
>
> LAMPINI
> He is now the Mayor of Riegelberg...

CONTINUED

47   CONTINUED

> NIEMANN
> (craftily)
> Oddly enough - that's where I --
> am going.
> (straight at Lampini)
> And, you, my friend, are going to
> help me get there.
>
> LAMPINI
> (not liking
> Niemann's manner)
> Riegelberg is a small village.
> The trip would be a loss...
>
> NIEMANN
> We'll go there, nevertheless...
>
> LAMPINI
> No, I say...
>
> NIEMANN
> Then Daniel and I - will go alone...

Terrified fear comes into Lampini's expression as he sees Niemann nod significantly to Daniel.

As the hunchback rises and his long arms reach slowly toward Lampini's throat, the old showman cringes in his chair.

> LAMPINI
> No, no...!

Daniel's talon-like fingers spread wide apart as they come closer and closer to Lampini's throat.

48   CLOSE SHOT - NIEMANN

Niemann's eyes gleam with a fanatical light as he looks unemotionally offscene, hearing Lampini's choked cry -- and then, a dying groan from the doomed man as the scene

                              DISSOLVES INTO

49   EXT. STORM CLOUDS - LONG SHOT - (STOCK) - NIGHT

The rain stops. The wind-swept clouds tear apart and the moon breaks through.

50   EXT. COUNTRYSIDE - ROAD - MED. LONG SHOT

Lampini's caravan is laboring up a rutty slope.

51   CLOSE SHOT - HIGH DRIVER'S SEAT OF FIRST VAN

The moonlight reveals that the driver is now - Daniel. Beside him sits Niemann. The hunchback is speaking.

> DANIEL
> When they search the ruins of the prison, our bodies will not be found. We should hide, somewhere...

> NIEMANN
> And so we shall -- but in the open...

Daniel doesn't understand. Niemann explains, with the tolerance he would show a child.

> NIEMANN (continues)
> We could ask for no safer place than where we are, friend Daniel -- I, as Lampini, you as my assistant...

A look of admiration appears on the hunchback's face as:

> NIEMANN (continues)
> All the protection of a traveling show, free to move on without question --
>   (his voice becomes harsh)
> -- but always and inexorably toward those for whom I have unloving memories...

> DANIEL
>   (purring)
> The ones who said you were - mad...?

> NIEMANN
> We will travel first to the village --

FAST DISSOLVE TO

52   EXT. COUNTRYSIDE - SIGN POST - CLOSE SHOT - <u>NIGHT</u>

The air is hazy with fog, but through it the legend below the arrow on the sign post is still readable:

RIEGELBERG - 1 km.

Over this, without interruption:

CONTINUED

52   CONTINUED

                    NIEMANN'S VOICE (continues)
          -- of Riegelberg --

                                        FAST DISSOLVE TO

53   EXT. HUSSMAN'S HOME - MED. SHOT - NIGHT

        The building reflects its medieval architecture. There
        is a thin haze of fog in the air.

        The DISSOLVE comes in on an ANGLE FROM THE GARDEN toward
        the open French windows - beyond which Hussman is seen
        seated at a chess table, the other player not yet revealed.
        Over this:

                    NIEMANN'S VOICE
                    (has continued without
                    interruption)
          -- where we will visit the Burgomaster,
          Ludwig Hussman...

        During this, the CAMERA has passed through the open
        doors of the window so that we are now in --

54   INT. HUSSMAN'S STUDY - MOVING SHOT - NIGHT

        -- where, as the CAMERA MOVES IN from the terrace,
        LUDWIG HUSSMAN is brought into a MEDIUM CLOSE SHOT. He
        is a man somewhere in his sixties, whose stern face and
        manner have been tempered by the passing years.

        His companion, INSPECTOR ARNZ, is a man of forty or so,
        attired in the uniform of the local police department.
        Both are deep in concentration over an "end game", which
        has narrowed down to just a few pieces.

                    HUSSMAN
          Your move, Inspector.

                    ARNZ
                    (moving his Queen)
          Check!

                    HUSSMAN
                    (moving his Bishop)
          Check -- and Queen.

                    ARNZ
          A very neat trap...
                    (he moves his King
                    out of "check")

                                        CONTINUED

54　CONTINUED

                    HUSSMAN
              (as he takes Arnz' Queen
               with his Bishop)
    Checkmate!
              (crowing)
    Put it in the book, Inspector!

Arnz takes a memo-book from his pocket and enters the lost game.

                    ARNZ
    As a man, I admire you -- as
    Burgomaster, I respect you --
              (kidding grimly)
    But as a chess-player, Herr Hussman,
    I _hate_ you!

                  RITA'S VOICE (o.s.)
    Granddad! Are you in --

55　MED. CLOSE SHOT - ENCLOSED STAIRWAY

RITA HOLT, Hussman's American-born granddaughter, races into view around the turn of the enclosed stairs. She is an attractive girl of about twenty.

                  RITA (continued)
    -- your study!?

She reaches the bottom of the stairs, looks o.s. - then turns to call to her husband, TONY HOLT, who is appearing on the landing above her. Tony is a typical American chap in his early thirties.

                  RITA (continued)
    He's here, Tony!

The CAMERA PANS with her as she runs across the room to where Hussman and Arnz are getting to their feet.

                  RITA (continued)
    Did you lose, Herr Arnz?
              (before he can answer)
    I'm sorry you did - but granddad always
    wins --
              (facing Hussman)
    -- don't you, you old darling!?
              (to Arnz, without pausing)
    I hope we're not breaking up your game,
    but Tony and I have decided --

                              CONTINUED

CONTINUED

> TONY
> (entering behind her)
> She means, she's decided --

> RITA
> (picking it up with a
> grim glance at Tony)
> -- to take in the midnight show of
> the Horror Exhibit that arrived in
> town this evening!
> (clawing the air in front
> of Hussman's face)
> Spooks! Ghouls! Vampires!
> (herself again)
> Get his coat and hat, Tony!
> (taking her grandfather's arm)
> You're going with us, darling!

> HUSSMAN
> To gawk at a lot of idiotic humbuggery...?
> (shaking his head)
> Not I, my dear -- I'm putting my weary
> bones where they belong -- in bed.

> RITA
> (with finality)
> Tony! His hat and coat!

> HUSSMAN
> I won't go!

> TONY
> Better give in - before she talks
> your ears off.
> (backing away as Rita
> whirls to face him)
> Now, now, darling! Remember your
> blood pressure!

> RITA
> (as he exits)
> Beast!
> (to her grandfather)
> That's the man I married! Talk, talk,
> talk! I can never get a word in edge-
> wise!
> (to Arnz)
> Come along, Inspector!

> ARNZ
> (very apologetically)
> Well, er, if you don't mind -- you
> see, I go on duty --
> (glancing at his watch)
> -- at midnight.

CONTINUED

55   CONTINUED - 2

>   HUSSMAN
>   (eyeing him, hard)
> Since <u>when</u>?
>
>   ARNZ
>   (blandly)
> A new departure, Herr Burgomaster --
> starting this evening...
>   (poking Russman)
> Checkmate!
>   (to Rita as he exits)
> Goodnight, Mrs. Holt!
>
>   HUSSMAN
> Bah!
>
>   RITA
>   (laughing)
> Never mind, granddad! I'll protect
> you!

Hussman sighs with resignation as Rita hauls him to where Tony is appearing with their hats and coats.

                              DISSOLVE INTO

56   EXT. LAMPINI'S TENTS - MED. CLOSE SHOT - BANNER - <u>NIGHT</u>

DISSOLVE in on an UPWARD ANGLE on the gaudy banner above the pergola entrance to the tent, on either side of which burn large oil lamps. On the banner, in fancy "side show" lettering, is the legend:

                Professor Bruno Lampini's
                   CHAMBER OF HORRORS

The CAMERA ANGLES DOWN to reveal Daniel, acting as ticket-seller. He is seated in the open belly of a weird looking papier-mache owl and, at the moment, is turning the handle which winds the spring of a hurdy-gurdy organ supplying appropriate music.

Several customers are coming out of the tent, huddling into their coats for protection against the penetrating fog from which Hussman, Rita and Tony now appear. As they join the villagers who are standing in line to buy tickets, the CAMERA MOVES UP.

>   RITA
> Br-r-r! I'm all over goose-pimples!

                                  CONTINUED

56   CONTINUED

> HUSSMAN
> (grumpily)
> Properly so, you little goose.
>
> RITA
> Don't be grouchy! This is _fun_!
>
> TONY
> Fun, she says.
>
> HUSSMAN
> (to Rita, as he shivers)
> How I let you drag me out in this fog, I'll never understand...
> (to Tony)
> You have my sympathy, young man.
>
> TONY
> Oh, she's all right --
> (pinching Rita's chin)
> -- after you get used to her.

He shys away from Rita's narrow look and steps to the ticket counter where the other customers are now moving toward the entrance.

> TONY (continued)
> (putting money on counter)
> Three.
>
> DANIEL
> Three. Straight ahead...
>
> TONY
> (taking Rita's arm)
> Come, my little pigeon! Shall we shiver, shake and shimmy, within?

Rita gives him a look as they exit into --

57   INT. EXHIBIT TENT - MED. PAN SHOT -

This square, moderately large tent is lighted with oil lamps placed so as to enhance the weird effect of the exhibits which are arranged along the walls. Beneath each is a card, identifying its particular "horror."

Our group ENTERS in a PAN SHOT, pausing at the first exhibit - a medieval "rack," on which a wax figure with an agonized expression is being "drawn and quartered" by another dummy who has his hands on the crank of the large wheel which, when turned, stretches the ropes tied to the sufferer's wrists and ankles. Its card carries the legend, "Medieval Quartering Rack."

CONTINUED

57   CONTINUED

                    TONY
          Remind me to buy one of those,
          sometime...

                    RITA
          For me, my sweet?

                    TONY
              (grimly)
          To stretch my salary check.

They move on toward the next exhibit....

58   CURTAINS OF DRACULA EXHIBIT - NIEMANN - CLOSE SHOT

The curtains draw apart slightly, revealing Niemann. His eyes bead with hatred as he sees and recognizes Hussman. As he withdraws his hands, the curtain closes.

59   CLOSE PAN SHOT - HUSSMAN, TONY AND RITA

The CAMERA PANS as they pass the next exhibit, without pausing.

                    RITA
          Tony! A cat with two heads!

                    TONY
          Ike and Mike --

                    RITA
          They look alike!

                    HUSSMAN
          Cheap fakery!

60   DRACULA EXHIBIT - MED. CLOSE SHOT

This is on the opposite side of the tent. As the show's "featured attraction", it is in a separate, curtain-inclosed booth raised a couple of feet above the ground.

Niemann, attired in Lampini's "Professor" outfit, is mounting to the platform. Since last seen, he has trimmed his hair and beard and appears quite a normal person. A small crucifix dangles from his watch chain.

                    NIEMANN
          This way, Ladies and Gentlemen!
          Step this way to gaze upon --

ac

61   FULL SHOT

The customers move toward the platform. Rita links her arm in Tony's and Hussman's and hauls them along gayly in the same direction. During this, we get a glimpse of the other "horrors" -- a boa-constrictor in the process of swallowing a zebra; an ancient instrument of torture, in which the victim lies sandwiched between two layers of iron spikes; a beheading-block, beside which stands an executioner holding by its hair the head of his last victim.

                    NIEMANN (continued)
          -- an exhibit absolutely without
          parallel in the realm of showmanship!
                    (as the customers crowd up)
          Among you, without doubt, are some --

62   CLOSE SHOT - HUSSMAN, TONY AND RITA

Rita and Tony are enjoying Niemann's spiel. Hussman, in CLOSE FOREGROUND, appears puzzled as he looks off toward Niemann.

                    NIEMANN'S VOICE (continues)
          -- who will question the truth of
          what I am going to say --

63   CLOSE SHOT - NIEMANN FROM HUSSMAN'S ANGLE

                    NIEMANN (continues)
          -- and the reality of what you are
          about to see...

64   CLOSE SHOT - HUSSMAN

He frowns as he tries to identify the familiar something he sees in the face of the speaker. Over this:

                    NIEMANN'S VOICE (continues)
          But believe me, my friends, this is
          no fake...

65   MED. SHOT - TOWARD PLATFORM

Niemann's hand pulls a cord which draws aside the curtains of the booth. The Dracula coffin is resting upon a table beside which stands Daniel, turning the crank of the mechanism which is tilting the coffin to an upright position

The ancient coffin is lined with tattered velvet, the pattern of which displays the Dracula Crest - a bat and a spike. This crest appears also on the outside of the coffin.

                                        CONTINUED

ac

65 CONTINUED

Earth fills the bottom of the box. Lying on it is the bleached, white skeleton, hair still on its head, with the disintegrating remains of its Inverness cape still in evidence. Through the thorax of the skeleton, where the heart once beat, a wooden stake has been driven into the earth beneath.

> NIEMANN (continued)
> Before your eyes is all that remains
> of a <u>vampire</u> --
> (Daniel exits)
> -- one of the world's undead, who,
> dared I remove this stake --
> (touches it)

66 CLOSE SHOT - RITA AND TONY

There is a scoffing smile on Tony's face. Rita is impressed and chilled.

> NIEMANN'S VOICE (continues)
> -- from where his heart once beat,
> would arise from the grave within
> which he lies and change into a bat --
> (facing his audience)
> -- a vampire bat which would feed
> hideously on the living --

67 MED. GROUP SHOT

A murmur of fear is heard from the superstitious villagers. Several exit, crossing themselves as:

> NIEMANN (continues)
> -- whose veins pulsate with warm and
> vibrant blood!

68 CLOSE SHOT - NIEMANN

He concludes with a flourish of his hand.

> NIEMANN
> Ladies and Gentlemen -- the actual
> skeleton of Count Dracula, the vampire!

69 CLOSE SHOT - RITA, TONY AND HUSSMAN

> HUSSMAN
> Rubbish!

CONTINUED

69 CONTINUED

>   RITA
> T-T-Tony! I - I'm scared!

>   TONY
>   (grinning)
> You asked for it, sweetheart...

70 MED. GROUP SHOT

The other frightened villagers are drifting out. Niemann, contemptuously amused, addresses Hussman.

>   NIEMANN
> You doubt what I say, Herr Burgomaster?

>   HUSSMAN
> Vampires! Bats! A stake, driven
> through a skeleton's heart! Silly
> gibberish - every word of it!

>   NIEMANN
>   (gesture)
> It is the only way in which a vampire
> can be made harmless, Herr Burgomaster...

>   HUSSMAN
>   (stepping closer)
> Who are you?

>   NIEMANN
>   (quietly, smiling)
> I am -- Lampini...

>   HUSSMAN
> You're not the Lampini I ran out of
> Visaria, three years ago...

>   NIEMANN
> That was my brother.
>   (sadly)
> He died -- recently.

71 CLOSE SHOT - HUSSMAN

>   HUSSMAN
>   (still puzzled)
> You seem to remind me of someone --
> someone I can't quite recall...

72   GROUP SHOT

> NIEMANN
> (shrugs, smiles)
> Perhaps you will remember -- later.
>
> HUSSMAN
> (frowning)
> Perhaps.
>
> RITA
> I've had enough, granddad --
>
> NIEMANN
> (closing the curtains)
> Goodnight, my friends...
>
> HUSSMAN
> Humph!

As Rita draws him and Tony toward the exit, the CAMERA MOVES UP to a CLOSE SHOT of Niemann. He looks after Hussman's exit for a moment of vengeful satisfaction -- then parts the curtains and steps into

73   DRACULA'S BOOTH - FULL SHOT

As the curtains close, Niemann steps closer to the coffin.

MOVING CLOSER AND CLOSER in a DOWNWARD ANGLE, the CAMERA STOPS as Niemann's hand comes into the picture and grasps the top of the stake. Moving this to and fro to loosen it from the hardened earth, Niemann's hand withdraws it --

74   CLOSE SHOT - NIEMANN

As he holds the stake poised over the exact spot from which he has withdrawn it, we see the start of Niemann's reaction as he stares down at --

75   DRACULA'S COFFIN - MED. CLOSE SHOT - DOWNWARD ANGLE

The skeleton is disappearing in a DISSOLVE which gives it body and restores its disintegrated clothing. Dracula opens his eyes slowly and stares up at --

76   CLOSER SHOT - NIEMANN - AS SEEN BY DRACULA

Niemann cannot wholly conceal his shock upon seeing Dracula's return to reality.

ac

77 CLOSE SHOT - DRACULA

His gaze shifts to the stake poised above his heart --
Then, toward Niemann. His eyes begin to glow in a
hypnotic stare.

> DRACULA
> Drop the stake from your hand...

78 MED. SHOT - NIEMANN AND COFFIN - IN AN ANGLE WHICH DOES
NOT SHOW DRACULA

As Niemann feels the force of Dracula's will, his fingers
start to release their grip upon the stake.

> DRACULA'S VOICE
> Drop it!

Just as it appears that Niemann will surrender to the
command, his free hand finds Lampini's watch chain. He
raises it, so that the Crucifix is directly in front of
Dracula's eyes.

79 CLOSE SHOT - DRACULA

> DRACULA
> (averting his face)
> No! No!
>
> NIEMANN'S VOICE
> The Crucifix, Count Dracula -- whose
> power over evil transcends even *your*
> hypnotic will...!
>
> DRACULA
> Take it from my sight!

80 CLOSEUP - NIEMANN

Triumphant, Niemann lowers the Crucifix as he presses
harder upon the stake until its pointed end almost
pierces Dracula's shirt front.

> NIEMANN (continues)
> I have done so...but if you move,
> I will send your soul --

The CAMERA PANS UP to Dracula's face as:

> NIEMANN'S VOICE (continues)
> -- back into the limbo of eternal
> waiting from which you have just
> returned --

ac

81   CLOSE SHOT - NIEMANN

The grim threat in his voice gives way to the manner of a crafty bargainer:

> NIEMANN (continued)
> -- But agree to help me and I will serve _you_...
> (leaning closer)
> Each day, at sundown...

82   CLOSE SHOT - DRACULA AS SEEN BY NIEMANN

Dracula's eyes glow with hope, as:

> NIEMANN'S VOICE (continues)
> -- and I will withdraw the stake from your heart, so that the nights may be yours...

83   CLOSE SHOT - NIEMANN

> NIEMANN (continues)
> Do as I ask, and I will protect the earth on which you lie - so that with the morning's sun, your grave will always be ready to receive you...

84   CLOSE SHOT - DRACULA

> DRACULA
> For that, I will do whatever you wish...

Niemann's hand is slowly raising the stake as the scene

DISSOLVES INTO

85   EXT. COUNTRYSIDE ROAD - HUSSMAN, RITA AND TONY - NIGHT

The CAMERA IS MOVING AHEAD of the trio through the fog. Rita is between the two men. Hussman, deeply thoughtful, is looking straight ahead.

> TONY
> You certainly picked a night for it, my pet...

> RITA (shivering)
> It's like being wrapped in the arms of a gigantic ghost...

CONTINUED

85   CONTINUED

                    HUSSMAN
               (assertively, to himself)
          I've seen that man, before.

                    RITA
          Professor Lampini?

Tony drops behind her a couple of steps. Sounds of a carriage rattling over the road behind them are heard.

                    HUSSMAN
          There's something about him I don't like.

                    RITA
          He isn't what you'd call a prize package --
               (turning to where Tony was)
          Is he, darl --
               (screams)
          Tony! Where are you?

                    TONY
               (touching her shoulder)
          Boo!

                    RITA
          Why do you do things like that!?

                    TONY
               (scoffingly)
          Fun. Says you
               (as the sounds of the
                approaching carriage
                become louder.)
          Listen!

They stop and look behind them toward --

86   COUNTRYSIDE ROAD - MED. LONG SHOT

A closed carriage emerges ghost-like from the fog, drawn by two swiftly moving horses. The driver is an old villager.

87   COUNTRYSIDE ROAD - MED. GROUP SHOT

Hussman and Rita step hurriedly off the road as the carriage clanks up and comes to a stop a few feet away. The door opens and Dracula steps out, with old-world politeness.

                    DRACULA
               (smiling)
          If you are going to Riegelberg --
               (stepping to one side)
          -- may I offer you the accommodation
          of my coach?

                                        CONTINUED

87   CONTINUED

>   TONY
>   You don't have to say _that_ twice!
>
>   DRACULA
>   Permit me...

He assists Hussman into the coach - and then Rita.

>   DRACULA
>   (to Tony)
>   After you...

As Tony steps into the coach and Dracula starts to follow, the scene

>   DISSOLVES INTO

88   INT. DRACULA'S CARRIAGE - CROSS ANGLE - FULL SHOT

On the left seat in the far corner is Dracula. Tony sits beside him. Hussman and Rita sit opposite. As the DISSOLVE comes in:

>   TONY
>   (is saying, to Dracula)
>   This is a hitch-hike, deluxe, if you
>   don't mind me saying so...
>
>   DRACULA
>   (politely puzzled)
>   Hitch-hike...?
>
>   TONY
>   You know -- snagging a lift --
>   American slang for being given a ride --
>   like you're giving us.
>
>   DRACULA
>   You're -- an American?
>
>   TONY
>   Oh, pardon me! I'm Tony Holt, U.S.A.
>   -- and this --
>   (smiling at Rita)
>   -- is my wife.
>   (grinning)
>   We're here on our honeymoon - visiting
>   her grandfather, Herr Hussman.

Dracula acknowledges the introduction with a bow.

                                              CONTINUED

88   CONTINUED

>   DRACULA
> Mrs. Holt...Herr Hussman...
>
>   HUSSMAN
>   (who has been concentrating)
> Eh? What?
>
>   DRACULA
> Permit me to introduce myself. I am
> Baron Latos - from Transylvania...
>
>   TONY
> Glad to know you, Baron.
>
>   DRACULA
> May I suggest that you join me in a
> bottle of wine, at the Inn...?

89   CLOSE SHOT - DRACULA

He addresses his next words to Rita.

>   DRACULA (continued)
>   (persuasively)
> In the nature of -- shall we say
> a little celebration, Mrs. Holt?

90   FULL GROUP SHOT

Rita's eyes become animated as she responds to Dracula's hypnotic suggestion.

>   DRACULA (continued)
>   (to Tony)
> My compliments -- to you and your
> charming wife...
>
>   TONY
> It's a deal! That is, if Herr Hussman...
>
>   HUSSMAN
> A glass of wine might warm my blood.
>   (to Dracula)
> But you will accept our hospitality,
> Baron...The wine of the country, from
> my cellar...
>
>   DRACULA
> Thank you, Herr Hussman...

On this, the scene

                                            DISSOLVES INTO

91 INT. HUSSMAN'S STUDY - CLOSE SHOT - WINE BOTTLE - <u>NIGHT</u>

The DISSOLVE comes in on a CLOSE SHOT, showing Tony's hand holding a wine bottle. He is refilling Dracula's glass as the CAMERA PULLS BACK into a LARGER SHOT, showing Dracula, Tony and Rita, seated near the table. Hussman, in his large chair, has dozed off. His chin has sagged down, upon his chest.

Tony is gay. Rita's eyes sparkle. She holds her glass up to look through it toward the light.

          RITA
Isn't it a beautiful color, Tony? It's red -- like blood...

Dracula's dark eyes glow, toward Rita. She flashes him a responsive smile.

          TONY
        (chiding Rita)
Hey! That vampire chatter has gone to your head!
        (pinching her cheek)
Or maybe, it's just the wine...
        (to Dracula)
Here's to you, Baron...You're a good scout.

He and Rita click their glasses and drink to Dracula. Tony drains his glass.

          DRACULA
Thank you...
        (raising his glass)
I drink to the future --
        (to Rita)
-- a union of souls,. Mrs. Holt -- to last throughout eternity -- a love free from all material needs.

          TONY
        (to Rita)
Poetic, isn't he?
        (to Dracula)
I'll drink to that lack of material needs...
        (discovering the bottle empty)
But not until I raid the wine-cellar, I won't...
        (rising)
'xcuse me, darling...Be right back, Baron...

Rita looks after Tony - then turns to Dracula. His gaze holds Rita, fascinated.

                              CONTINUED

91   CONTINUED

Dracula, resting his elbows upon the table, brings his hands together so that the ring upon a finger of his right hand is almost directly in front of Rita....

92   CLOSE SHOT - DRACULA

His eyes stare fixedly in Rita's direction - then drop to the ring. The metal band begins to glow...

93   CLOSE SHOT - RITA

Hypnotically directed, Rita's eyes lower until the line of her vision is directly toward --

94   CLOSE SHOT - DRACULA'S HANDS

He turns the ring upon his finger so that the signet portion, exhibiting the Dracula crest, is brought into view. This part glows even brighter than the band.

95   CLOSE SHOT - DRACULA AND RITA

Dracula raises his eyes. Simultaneously, Rita raises hers. Their gazes meet. Slowly, Dracula removes the ring from his finger. Responsive to his will, Rita extends her hand. Dracula slips the ring upon her finger, turning it so that the signet portion is beneath.

>   RITA
> It's too - large.
>
>   DRACULA
> It will become smaller.

96   CLOSE SHOT - RITA'S AND DRACULA'S HANDS

The ring shrinks to a snug fit around Rita's finger.

97   CLOSE SHOT - RITA AND DRACULA

Dracula raises his eyes from their hands. Simultaneously, as before, Rita raises hers. She smiles, as from far away

>   DRACULA
>   (in a low voice)
> I will come for you - before the dawn.

CONTINUED

97 CONTINUED

>   RITA
>   (almost inaudibly)
>   I will be waiting...

Their gazes continue to hold....

98 CLOSE SHOT - HUSSMAN

As his head falls over to one side, Hussman awakens with an embarrassed effort to cover the fact that he has been asleep.

>   HUSSMAN
>   And as I was saying....
>   (stopping)
>   To be truthful, I've been asleep --

99 GROUP SHOT

Rita looks at her grandfather with a vague smile.

>   HUSSMAN (continued)
>   (apologetically)
>   -- and I haven't the remotest idea
>   what I was saying. I apologize, Baron....
>
>   DRACULA
>   (graciously)
>   It's quite all right...
>   (smiling at Rita)
>   Mr. and Mrs. Holt have been telling
>   me about their home, in America....

Tony enters, carrying a cob-webby bottle of wine.

>   TONY
>   Here we are!
>
>   DRACULA
>   (rising)
>   I didn't realize it, but we have talked
>   almost until dawn...I must leave you now...
>   (smiling at Rita)
>   It has been a charming evening...
>   (to Tony)
>   From what you say, America is a country
>   of strong and vigorous people --
>   (as they shake hands)
>   I think I shall visit it, sometime...

CONTINUED

99 CONTINUED

>   TONY
> When you do, let me know - and
> I'll meet you at the station
> with a brass band...

>   HUSSMAN
> Goodnight, Baron...

>   DRACULA
>   (bowing)
> Thank you, Herr Hussman, for your
> hospitality...

As he and Tony start toward the exit, the CAMERA MOVES UP CLOSER, to Rita. She looks after Dracula for a moment, drops her eyes to the ring upon her finger - then turns toward the stair alcove.

>   HUSSMAN'S VOICE
> Aren't you going to tell me goodnight...?

100 LARGER SHOT

Tony and Dracula have exited. Hussman is looking after Rita. She pauses an instant, with a trace of a smile.

>   RITA
> Goodnight, granddad....

She continues toward the stair alcove...

101 CLOSE SHOT - HUSSMAN

He senses something odd in Rita's manner, but dismisses it as he turns away and starts toward his old-fashioned "secretary" desk.

102 EXT. STREET IN FRONT OF HUSSMAN'S HOME - MED. SHOT - <u>NIGHT</u>

The carriage is still waiting. The driver is asleep on the high seat, his chin resting upon his breast. Dracula is coming from the house and Tony is standing in the doorway.

>   TONY
> See you again, Baron... It's been a
> swell party...

>   DRACULA
> Thank you, Mr. Holt.

CONTINUED

102 CONTINUED

As the door closes behind Tony, the CAMERA MOVES UP to a CLOSER SHOT of Dracula, at the carriage.

          DRACULA
        (sharply)
Driver!

          DRIVER
        (coming out of his doze)
Eh? What?
        (hopping down)
Sorry, sir - but it's been a long wait...
        (starts to open door)

          DRACULA
Just a moment...
        (the driver turns,
         to look at him)

103 CLOSE SHOT - DRACULA

His eyes glow as he fixes them upon the driver's in a steady, hypnotic gaze...

104 CLOSE SHOT - DRIVER

As he comes under the influence of Dracula's will, the driver closes his eyes for a moment - then opens them.

          DRACULA
        (quietly, commandingly)
Go to your home and sleep...You will find your carriage in front of the Inn, tomorrow morning...

Responsive to Dracula's will, the driver touches his cap and EXITS. Dracula starts toward the front of the cab...

105 INT. HUSSMAN'S STUDY - MED. SHOT - <u>NIGHT</u>

Hussman is standing at his desk, rummaging through a drawer. Tony, who has opened the second bottle of wine, is downing a "nightcap".

          TONY
Better get some sleep, Granddad...

          HUSSMAN
Right away, my boy...

          TONY
        (exiting up stairs)
'night....

bm

106 CLOSE SHOT - HUSSMAN - AT DESK

Deep in thought as he tries to recall where he has seen "Lampini's" face, he takes several old records books from one of the drawers and starts to thumb through them....

107 INT. TONY'S AND RITA'S BEDROOM - MED. FULL SHOT - <u>NIGHT</u>

There is only one light burning - a table lamp. Rita is in the center of the room, looking with fascinated eyes at the Dracula ring as the door opens and Tony enters.

>   TONY
>   (gaily)
>   It turned out to be fun after all,
>   didn't it, m'pet...?
>
>   RITA
>   (far away)
>   I -- I seem to be moving --
>   (closing her eyes
>   for a second)
>   -- in a dream...
>
>   TONY
>   (crossing to her)
>   Look not upon the wine when it is red!

108 CLOSER SHOT - TONY AND RITA

As Tony reaches Rita, she looks at him, smiling strangely.

>   RITA
>   (quoting Dracula, softly)
>   '....To live throughout eternity,
>   without material needs...'
>
>   TONY
>   (mystified and alarmed)
>   Hey! You'd better lie down!
>
>   RITA
>   My ring hurts me...

She closes her eyes and sways. Tony grabs her hand and looks at --

109 CLOSE SHOT - RITA'S AND TONY'S HANDS

The band of metal has tightened about Rita's finger until it appears swollen. Tony's hand turns hers over, revealing--

bm

110   VERY CLOSEUP - RING

-- showing the Dracula crest....

111   CLOSE SHOT - RITA AND TONY

Tony stares at the ring with increasing alarm..

    TONY
 The Dracula crest! The same as the
 one on that coffin!
    (seizing Rita's arm)
 Where'd you get it!?

    RITA
    (dreamily)
 Baron Latos -- gave it to me...
    (a sudden sob)
 Get it off, Tony! Get it off!

Tony tries to do so, but the ring is too tight.

    TONY
    (completely sobered)
 Now don't get excited, darling!
 We'll try soap and water...!

He draws her along with him toward the old-fashioned bowl-and-pitcher washstand...

112   INT. HUSSMAN'S STUDY - CLOSE SHOT - NEAR DESK

Hussman, thumbing through the pages of one of the older books, finds an entry which brings a startled exclamation.

    HUSSMAN
 Niemann! Of course! Doctor Niemann!

113   EXT. GARDEN OF HUSSMAN'S HOME - MED. SHOT

An eerie quality comes into the score as a portion of the fog spirals itself into a materialization of Dracula, walking toward CAMERA. Pausing in MED. CLOSE FOREGROUND, Dracula directs his glowing eyes in the direction of --

114   VERANDA OF HUSSMAN'S HOME - MED. SHOT

In an ANGLE FROM BEHIND DRACULA, Hussman can be seen standing at the desk in the study, looking at the book ---

bm

115   INT. HUSSMAN'S STUDY - HUSSMAN AT DESK - CLOSE SHOT

The old man closes his eyes and shakes his head, as though to clear his suddenly befuddled mind.

116   EXT. GARDEN OF HUSSMAN'S HOME - DRACULA - CLOSE SHOT

The hypnotic glow in Dracula's eyes becomes stronger...

117   INT. HUSSMAN'S STUDY - NEAR DESK - MED. CLOSE

Hussman opens his eyes and draws his hand across his face as though to throw off the unaccountable depression which has seized him as he moves in a PAN SHOT toward the closed veranda doors.

Opening them wide, he turns away and staggers like a drunken man to a chair, in which he collapses weakly.

118   CLOSE SHOT - HUSSMAN

As he tries to throw off his feelings of depression, he becomes aware of a fluttering sound - the sound of wings, beating the air. He tenses forward, turning his eyes toward --

119   MED. SHOT THROUGH VERANDA DOORS INTO GARDEN

Materializing out of the fog which almost obscures the garden, a giant bat is winging its way toward the doors.

120   CLOSE SHOT - HUSSMAN

As he sees this repulsive horror flying toward him out of the fog, Hussman's eyes dilate in silent, fascinated terror.

The sound of the beating wings becomes louder. On the wall behind Hussman appears the shadow of the bat - upon whose off-scene form Hussman's horror-stricken eyes are fixed as the scene

                                                DISSOLVES INTO

121   INT. TONY'S AND RITA'S BEDROOM - CLOSE SHOT - WASH-BASIN

As the scene DISSOLVES IN, Rita's hand, held by Tony's, is seen in the soapy water. Tony, rubbing her finger with the soft bar of soap, gets some of it around and under the ring and, as the CAMERA PULLS BACK into a LARGER SHOT, tries to twist the ring from her finger.

                    RITA
          It hurts!

She draws her hand away, staring at the ring, trying to get it off.

                    RITA
                (hysterically)
          Tony! Tony!

                    TONY
          Steady, sweetheart! I'll go down-
          stairs and get a pair of pliers, to
          cut it off...!
                (frantically)
          And don't leave this room! Do you
          understand!? Don't leave this room...!

He runs toward the door...

122   CLOSE SHOT - RITA

Rita, still trying to remove the ring, suddenly becomes calmer. Drying her fingers on a towel, she holds her hand up, turning it this way and that, looking at the ring.

As her manner becomes still calmer, her eyes fix upon the metal band, hypnotically fascinated....

123   INT. HUSSMAN'S STUDY - MED. SHOT - TOWARD STAIR ALCOVE

As Tony dashes down the stairs into the room, he stops suddenly as he sees Hussman's body, lying on the floor, partially concealed by the chair. Alarmed, he runs toward FOREGROUND and stoops down to make a hurried examination, his reaction to Hussman's silent heart being proof that the old man is dead.

Suddenly, Tony takes a sharper reaction, bending closer to look at --

124. CLOSEUP - HUSSMAN'S HEAD

His eyes are closed, and his head is turned AWAY FROM THE CAMERA. The collar of his shirt has been torn open - revealing two puncture-like marks on the side of his throat near the jugular vein.

125. MED. CLOSE SHOT

Horrified, Tony springs to his feet and, in a PAN SHOT, runs across the room to the desk. He grabs the telephone from its cradle and jiggles the hook several times.

    TONY
   (when the operator answers)
 Connect me with Inspector Arnz! Hurry!

126. INT. ARNZ' BEDROOM - (PICKUP) - CLOSE SHOT - NEAR BED

The telephone on the small table beside the bed starts ringing as the CAMERA PULLS BACK into a MEDIUM CLOSE SHOT. Arnz wakes up, snaps on the bed-table lamp and reaches sleepily for the telephone.

    ARNZ
 Hello...
   (politely puzzled)
 Oh, yes, Mr. Holt...
   (takes a terrific reaction)
 The Burgomaster!?
   (shocked, he continues to
    listen; then)
 Wounds on his neck? What kind of wounds?

127. INT. HUSSMAN'S STUDY - NEAR PHONE - TONY - CLOSE SHOT

    TONY
 Two small punctures -- like teeth-marks...
   (a slight pause)
 Yes, Inspector - that _is_ what I think...

128. INT. ARNZ' BEDROOM - ARNZ - CLOSE SHOT .

    ARNZ
   (crisply)
 I'll be over right away...

129. INT. HUSSMAN'S STUDY - NEAR PHONE - TONY - CLOSE SHOT

    TONY
 That would only waste time! There's something we should do without a moment's delay....

130 INT. TONY'S AND RITA'S BEDROOM - MED. SHOT

Rita is pacing to and fro. Suddenly aware of a CHANGE in the ring, she stops abruptly and stares at her hand.

131 CLOSEUP - RITA'S HAND

The Dracula ring is beginning to glow. As it becomes brighter and brighter, the MUSIC MODULATES into the eerie Dracula theme, and the CAMERA PULLS BACK into a LARGER SHOT which shows a slow change coming over Rita's face...

The terror of a moment ago departs, replaced by a sense of exhilaration as she stares, fascinated, at the ring...

132 INT. HUSSMAN'S STUDY - NEAR PHONE - TONY - CLOSE SHOT

> TONY
> That's right, Inspector! I'll lock Mrs. Holt in her room and leave right away! Get your men together - I'll meet you there...

He bangs the receiver into its cradle and starts hurriedly toward the stairs...

133 INT. RITA'S AND TONY'S BEDROOM - MED. CLOSE

Rita turns suddenly and moves toward the French doors, opening them wide.

134 EXT. GARDEN OF HUSSMAN'S HOME - BEDROOM BALCONY - MED. CLOSE SHOT

As Rita steps out onto the balcony, the CAMERA PULLS BACK and ANGLES with her as she descends the stairs. Moving like a person in a dream, she becomes a wraith-like figure as she walks through the fog toward where Dracula comes into view, waiting.

135 INT. TONY'S AND RITA'S BEDROOM - FULL SHOT

Tony rushes in, stopped by paralyzing fear as he sees the deserted room. He runs across the room and exits through the doors into --

136 EXT. GARDEN OF HUSSMAN'S HOME - BEDROOM BALCONY - TONY

Tony comes onto the balcony, reacting in frozen horror --

bm

137   GARDEN - FULL SHOT - FROM BALCONY ANGLE

Rita's ghost-like figure is dimly seen as she moves toward Dracula...

138   BALCONY - PAN SHOT - TONY

Tony races down the stairs. The CAMERA PANS with him as he runs across the garden.

                    TONY
    Rita!

139   MED. SHOT - DRACULA AND RITA

As though Rita hadn't heard Tony, she moves toward Dracula, her eyes meeting his in an unbreakable fascination. As they walk toward the background, they <u>dematerialize</u>, into ghost-like figures -- and vanish...

140   CLOSE SHOT - TONY

Driven almost insane, Tony runs in a PAN SHOT toward the point where Rita and Dracula disappeared

141   MED. CLOSE NEAR TREE

Tony comes to a helpless stop. He is like a demented person as his eyes try to pierce the fog.

                    TONY
    Rita! Rita!

He is plunging into the enveloping fog as the scene

                            DISSOLVES INTO

142   EXT. OUTSKIRTS OF VILLAGE - CARAVAN - MED. SHOT - <u>MORNING</u>

The fog has become an early morning mist, through which are seen the bulking shapes of the Lampini vehicles. The restless horses are in harness and the vehicles are coupled together, ready for the road. Daniel is seen, dozing in the high seat of the leading van...

143   CLOSE SHOT - DANIEL

The reins lie loosely in his hands, upon his lap...

From offscene come the sounds of men, running - and unintelligible voices.

Daniel opens his eyes and looks off toward --

44 NEAR ROAD - MED. LONG SHOT THROUGH TREES

Tony and Arnz with two or three of Arnz' men in uniform and four or five villagers, have left the road behind them and are short-cutting through the trees in the direction of the caravan.

45 VAN OF LAMPINI CARAVAN - MED. CLOSE

Reacting, Daniel swings himself out of the seat to the ground and runs in a PAN SHOT toward the rear of the living-wagon. He bangs loudly on the door...

46 AMONG TREES - MED. GROUP SHOT

Tony, Arnz and the others are now closer than before...

47 REAR OF LIVING-WAGON - MED. CLOSE SHOT

Niemann is appearing from within the wagon. He hears the men.

      DANIEL
  Master! They're after us...!

Niemann takes one fast look - then starts in a run toward the front of the caravan, followed by the fear-stricken Daniel.

48 AMONG TREES - MED. CLOSE GROUP SHOT

Tony, Arnz and the others are running in a SWINGING PAN SHOT toward the caravan.

49 NEAR FIRST VAN OF CARAVAN - MED. SHOT

Niemann and Daniel are climbing into the driver's seat. Niemann cracks the whip over the horses' backs...

50 AMONG TREES - MED. CLOSE GROUP SHOT

Tony, Arnz and the others react as they see the departing caravan.

51 CARAVAN - MED. FULL SHOT

The caravan is gathering speed down the road as Niemann furiously lashes the horses....

152 TONY, ARNZ AND VILLAGERS - MED. SHOT

The CAMERA SWINGS with them as they come to a breathless stop in f.g., looking after the caravan...

153 CARAVAN - MED. LONG SHOT

The vehicles are being swallowed up in the hazy mist just as Dracula's carriage comes plunging into view from across the open field and swings onto the road...

154 CLOSE SHOT - DRACULA'S CARRIAGE

Dracula is on the high seat, lashing the horses into furious pursuit after the caravan, ahead...

155 TONY, ARNZ AND VILLAGERS - MED. CLOSE SHOT

TONY
(frantically)
My wife's in that carriage!

He and the others start out in a run, as the scene

DISSOLVES INTO

156 EXT. COUNTRYSIDE ROAD - LONG SHOT - EARLY MORNING

The fog has dissipated into an over-lying haze through which the road, in the semi-distance, is obscured as though through a cloudy glass.

Drawn by the furiously driven horses, are seen the vehicles of the Lampini caravan. Some distance behind it and gaining slowly in pursuit, is Dracula's carriage.

157 INT. DRIVER'S SEAT OF LAMPINI VAN - CLOSE SHOT

Niemann, driving with reckless fury, lashes the horses into greater speed. Daniel sits beside him.

158 EXT. COUNTRYSIDE ROAD - DRACULA'S CARRIAGE

Dracula cracks his whip as the CAMERA PANS with the carriage when it comes through foreground.

159 INT. DRACULA'S CARRIAGE - FULL SHOT

Rita is in the rear seat. There is a peculiar out-of-this-world smile upon her face as she stares straight

CONTINUED

59 CONTINUED

ahead of her.

60 EXT. COUNTRYSIDE ROAD - DRACULA'S CARRIAGE - PAN SHOT

Dracula cracks his whip across the horses' flanks.

61 COUNTRYSIDE ROAD - LONG PAN SHOT

Dracula's carriage is gaining on the caravan...

62 CREST OF HILL - MED. SHOT

ANGLE UP THE SLOPE OF THE HILL as Tony, Arnz and the other men appear over the crest and come to a stop, reacting to the vehicles in the distance.

163 LONG PAN SHOT - CARAVAN AND DRACULA'S CARRIAGE

A FLASH of the pursuit, as seen by Tony, et al.

164 CREST OF HILL - MED. GROUP SHOT

As the men start down the slope pell-mell, Arnz draws his pistol and fires toward Dracula's carriage.

              TONY
    Bullets won't kill him! We've got
    to drive a stake through his heart!

The CAMERA PANS as Arnz follows Tony in his reckless, head-long plunge down the slope.

165 INT. LAMPINI'S VAN - DRIVER'S SEAT - CLOSE SHOT

Niemann and Daniel are looking off toward --

166 EXT. HILLSIDE - MED. LONG SHOT

Tony, Arnz and the others are tearing down the hillside.

167 INT. DRIVER'S SEAT OF LAMPINI VAN - CLOSE SHOT

              DANIEL
    They'll kill us, Master! They'll
    kill us!

CONTINUED

167   CONTINUED

                    NIEMANN
           I know how to stop them!

       He hands the reins to Daniel and starts to climb into
       the compartment, behind them....

168   EXT. COUNTRYSIDE ROAD - LONG SHOT

       Dracula's carriage continues to gain on the Lampini
       vehicles.

169   EXT. DRACULA'S CARRIAGE - CLOSE SHOT - DRACULA

       Dracula is in a frenzy of fear that dawn will catch him
       away from his grave. He looks off, toward --

170   EXT. HORIZON - LONG SHOT - (STOCK) - <u>EARLY MORNING</u>

       The brilliant rim of the morning's sun breaks through ---

171   EXT. DRACULA'S CARRIAGE - CLOSE SHOT - DRACULA

       His eyes dilate in terror as he sees the sun.

172   INT. DRACULA'S CARRIAGE - FULL SHOT

       Rita sits as before, staring into distant space.

173   EXT. DRACULA'S CARRIAGE - CLOSE SHOT - DRACULA

       As the sunlight falls upon him, Dracula's eyes start to
       close. As the catalepsy comes upon him, his hands drop
       the reins...

174   MED. LONG SHOT - DRACULA'S CARRIAGE

       With no one at the reins, the galloping horses swerve
       off the road and the front wheels of the carriage hit
       a deep rut...

175   CLOSE SHOT - FRONT WHEELS OF CARRIAGE

       As the wheels fall into the rut, the king pin flies out of
       its socket...

176   EXT. HILLSIDE - CLOSE PAN SHOT - TONY

The CAMERA SWINGS WITH HIM as he comes to a horrified stop, stunned, as he sees ---

177   MED. LONG SHOT - DRACULA'S CARRIAGE

The horses continue onward as the carriage leaves the road, throwing Dracula's body into the air...The carriage continues rolling a little distance, then overturns...

178   HILLSIDE - CLOSE SHOT - TONY

Frantic with fear that Rita has been killed, Tony plunges down the hillside in a PAN SHOT toward the road...

179   LAMPINI CARAVAN - MED. SHOT - BETWEEN VAN AND LIVING-WAGON

One of the van doors has been opened from the inside, Niemann, holding the Dracula coffin balanced on one end, gives it a mighty shove...

180   MED. CLOSE - ROAD

Dracula's coffin comes flying from the space between the van and the living-wagon. It hits the road and breaks into a shower of splinters and dust...

181   MED. SHOT - DRACULA'S CARRIAGE

Dracula's body, lying on the ground some distance from the overturned vehicle, appears as if dead.

Tony runs in, climbs into the wreck of the carriage and lifts Rita's inert body in his arms...

182   HILLSIDE - MED. PAN SHOT

The CAMERA ANGLES with Arnz and the others as they pour down the hill onto the road.

The villagers shout as they pick up rocks and hurl them toward the caravan, while Arnz and his men run out toward the wrecked carriage...

1c

183   OFF ROAD - NEAR WRECKED CARRIAGE

Tony, carrying Rita's limp body, is coming toward a tree in CLOSE FOREGROUND, as Arnz and his men come running toward the carriage.

The villagers, upscene, seeing that further pursuit of the caravan is useless, now run back toward Dracula's body...

> ARNZ
> Is she all right, Mr. Holt?

> TONY
> She's alive...
> (looking up)
> Drive a stake through Dracula's heart!

Arnz and his men exit toward the carriage...

184   CARRIAGE - FULL SHOT

Arnz and his men follow the excited villagers who have picked up Dracula's body and are starting with it toward a gully...

185   CLOSE SHOT - TONY

Tony, chafing Rita's hands, sees the ring still on her finger. He tries to remove it.

186   CLOSE SHOT - TONY'S AND RITA'S HANDS

The ring appears imbedded in the flesh of Rita's finger.

187   CLOSE SHOT - TONY

Panic seizes him - the dread fear that Rita has been lost to Dracula, forever.

> TONY
> Rita! Come back to me! Come back...!

He looks offscene, reacting to --

188   MED. LONG SHOT - GROUP FROM TONY'S ANGLE

The villagers are putting Dracula's body in the gully. Arnz picks up a sharply pointed piece of branchwood and holds it upright over the unseen body. One of his men picks up a large rock and raises it into the air above the stake....

189   CLOSE GROUP SHOT - VILLAGERS

Several of them turn away and cross themselves as, from offscene, come dull thudding sounds of the stake being driven home.

190   MED. DOWNWARD ANGLE - IN GULLY

The stake has been driven home. As Arnz and his men step back, Dracula's body DISSOLVES INTO its skeleton.

191   GROUP SHOT - VILLAGERS

They react with superstitious awe and cross themselves --

192   MED. SHOT - UNDER TREE

Rita still lies motionless, supported in Tony's arms.

As the CAMERA MOVES forward until they are in a CLOSEUP, Tony takes Rita's hand, staring at it with returning hope as he sees...

193   CLOSEUP - TONY'S AND RITA'S HANDS

Dracula's ring dematerializes and disappears....

194   CLOSEUP - TONY AND RITA

Rita's eyes open. Slowly, as she looks up at Tony, a smile of recognition comes into her face.

> RITA
> Oh, Tony! I've had such a horrible dream!
> (she clings to him sobbing in relief)
>
> TONY
> It's all right now, darling --

As he holds her close to him, the scene

DISSOLVES INTO

195   COUNTRYSIDE - LONG PAN SHOT

    The Lampini caravan thunders recklessly down a grade.

                                                DISSOLVE INTO

196   MONTAGE: to be composed of fast DISSOLVES AND WIPES

    a. EXT. CLOSE SHOT - DAY
        Furiously galloping horses.

    b. EXT. CLOSE SHOT - DAY
        Distortion angle on wagon wheels, turning fast.

    c. EXT. SIGN POST - DAY
        FAST PAN SHOT on a roadsign, the arrow on which
        indicates: FRANKENSTEIN, 80 km.

    d. EXT. DRIVING SEAT OF VAN - CLOSE SHOT - DANIEL AND
        NIEMANN - DAY
        Niemann, who is driving, lashes the horses furiously.

    e. EXT. CLOSE SHOT - DAY
        Another shot of galloping horses, CLOSER than before.

    f. EXT. CLOSE SHOT - DAY
        Another PAN ANGLE ON wagon wheels.

    g. EXT. SIGN POST - DAY
        PAN on another roadsign, whose arrow indicates that
        Frankenstein is now only 30 km. distant.

    h. EXT. COUNTRYSIDE - MED. LONG SHOT - DAY
        PAN with the caravan, moving at more normal speed.

    i. EXT. CLOSE SHOT - DAY
        CLOSE ANGLE on horses' legs as they strain up a
        heavy grade.

    j. EXT. CLOSE SHOT - DAY
        Another PAN ANGLE on wagon wheels, turning slowly.

    k. EXT. SIGN POST - DAY
        PAN ANGLE on another sign, whose arrow indicates that
        Frankenstein is now only 1 km. away as the MONTAGE
        ends and DISSOLVES INTO -

197   EXT. COUNTRYSIDE - MED. FULL SHOT - DAY

    Obscured somewhat by the early morning haze, the little
    Village of Frankenstein lies dozing in the semi-distance.

                                                CONTINUED

1c

197   CONTINUED

Near some trees are a couple of Gipsy living-wagons. The horses are tethered, nearby. A dozen or so villagers, together with several children, are watching a girl who is dancing to music supplied by four other Gipsies, two men and two women.

Beyond this activity is the Lampini caravan. The contents of the van lie scattered about. The tent has been erected, and Niemann and Daniel are putting the papier-mache owl in place in the pergola.

198   MED. CLOSE SHOT - DANCING GIRL

Her name is ILONKA. ANGLE to feature her as she dances in a PAN SHOT which brings the other Gipsies into view. The leader, named FEJOS, is a surly-appearing fellow of middle age. His wife, URLA, is a typical Gipsy shrew. The other couple, a man and a girl, are somewhat younger - but the girl is hard and coarse compared to Ilonka, who is gay, vivacious and pretty.

199   LAMPINI TENT - MED. CLOSE SHOT

As Niemann and Daniel complete the installation of the owl, Niemann exits toward the van. Daniel, coming toward CAMERA, stops in CLOSE FOREGROUND and looks off at --

200   MED. CLOSE SHOT - ILONKA

-- as seen from Daniel's angle. Her dark eyes sparkle and flash as she dances with inherent, joyful abandon.

201   CLOSE SHOT - DANIEL

Ilonka's beauty holds the hunchback fascinated.

202   CLOSER SHOT - ILONKA

Her dancing becomes faster and faster as the tempo of the music increases.

203   CLOSE SHOT - DANIEL

As he watches Ilonka, the hunchback's face softens into an almost human smile.

204   MED. FULL SHOT - ILONKA AND MUSICIANS

As the music approaches its climax, two men of Frankenstein's Police Department enter and move toward the musicians. The spokesman of this pair is INSPECTOR GERLACH.

205   MED. CLOSE SHOT - MUSICIANS AND OFFICERS

Fejos and the others are unaware that Gerlach and his companion have entered and are standing nearby, waiting for the dance to end.

206   MED. CLOSE SHOT - DANIEL

Still fascinated, Daniel is brought back to reality as Niemann touches him upon the shoulder and indicates that he is to help him carry the props into the tent. Daniel is looking over his shoulder for a last glimpse of Ilonka as he follows Niemann out of scene.

207   MED. SHOT - MUSICIANS AND OFFICERS

Ilonka's abandoned dance concludes as the wild strains of the music climax and end.

Two or three villagers toss small coins at Ilonka's feet and applaud enthusiastically.

As Ilonka blows gay kisses toward them and picks up the money, the CAMERA MOVES toward Gerlach and the other Gipsies. Fejos, seeing the law, begins to fawn.

> FEJOS
> You think Ilonka is pretty, yes...?
> For a few pfennig, she will dance again.
>
> GERLACH
> Not in the Village of Frankenstein, she won't!
> (eyeing Fejos)
> We've had nothing but stealing since you came here -- the Burgomaster says you're to move on, immediately.
>
> FEJOS
> But, Herr Inspector ---
>
> GERLACH
> No arguments! Break camp and get out!
> (to the villagers)
> There'll be no horror show, either -- you may as well go home.

CONTINUED

207   CONTINUED

The villagers begin to disperse. Gerlach and his companion are moving toward the Lampini vehicles as Urla and the two other Gipsies join Fejos, whose face takes on an expression of sullen rage.

208   LAMPINI TENT - MED. SHOT

Niemann and Daniel are carrying one of the cases toward the tent as Gerlach and his companion enter.

> GERLACH
> Just a moment, Lampini!

Niemann and Daniel stop in foreground and lower the case to the ground as Gerlach and his companion enter.

> GERLACH (continues)
> The Burgomaster won't grant you a
> permit -- so pack up and be on your way.
>
> NIEMANN
> But why? There's nothing in my Exhibit
> to offend anyone...
>
> GERLACH
> We've had enough horrors around here...
>   (indicating the direction)
> Do you see those ruins...?
>   (as Niemann looks off)
> Our village has been quiet and peaceful
> since the dam broke --

209   LONG SHOT - TOWARD HILL

Below the unrepaired dam, the skeletal outlines of the Frankenstein ruins stand out in gaunt silhouette against the afternoon sky. Over this:

> GERLACH'S VOICE (continues)
> -- and swept the Wolf Man and the
> Frankenstein Monster to their
> destruction, several years ago...

210   LAMPINI TENT - GROUP SHOT

Niemann and Daniel are looking off toward the ruins as:

> GERLACH (continues)
> No one mentions that place - nor does
> anyone ever go near it ...
>   (as Niemann faces him)
> That's why you can't exhibit here,
> Lampini -- we want nothing to remind
> us of something we're trying to forget....

CONTINUED

210   CONTINUED

                    NIEMANN
            We've come a long way - it is late, and
            my horses are tired...May we rest here,
            until morning?

                    GERLACH
            I suppose so - but you'll have to ask
            the Burgomaster. Come along...

                    NIEMANN
                    (to Daniel)
            Start loading...

        As Niemann exits with the two men, Daniel picks up the
        packing case and starts toward the van as the scene

                                        DISSOLVES INTO

211   GIPSY WAGONS - MED. SHOT - <u>DUSK</u>

        The Gipsies have broken camp. One of the wagons is on
        its way out, driven by the younger man and woman. Fejos
        is harnessing the horse to the second wagon, while his
        wife and Ilonka finish loading.

        As Fejos completes the harnessing, he picks up his heavy-
        handled whip and starts toward the rear of the wagon.
        The CAMERA MOVES UP into a CLOSER SHOT.

                    FEJOS
                    (scowling at Ilonka)
            Hand over the money the villagers gave you...

                    ILONKA
                    (taking coins from pocket)
            Only your share...

                    FEJOS
            All of it!

                    ILONKA
                    (flaring)
            When I joined you, it was agreed that
            I keep half!

                    FEJOS
            Give me that money!

212   LAMPINI VAN - MED. CLOSE SHOT

        Daniel, who has just loaded a box into the van, turns to
        look off toward the Gipsy wagon as:

                                        CONTINUED

212 CONTINUED

> ILONKA'S VOICE
> (rises higher and higher)
> If you try to rob me, I'll tell the
> Police that...

213 GIPSY WAGON - MED. CLOSE SHOT

Daniel, seen in the background, leaves the van and starts downscene as:

> ILONKA (continues)
> -- you're the one who's been doing the stealing around here!

> FEJOS
> I'll thrash you within an inch of your life!

He grabs Ilonka's wrist. She frees herself with a jerk and throws the coins into his face as she starts at him, pummeling and clawing like a little wildcat.

> ILONKA
> You smelly pig!

Fejos flings Ilonka away and swings the butt of his whip at her head.

214 CLOSE SHOT - DANIEL

As he reacts to what he has seen, Daniel starts running in a PAN SHOT which brings the Gipsy wagon into view and shows Fejos lashing Ilonka, motionless upon the ground.

215 CLOSE SHOT - FEJOS AND URLA

In an ANGLE which does not include Ilonka's body, Fejos, infuriated, is lashing her with his whip.

Urla, looking off, sees Daniel coming toward them. She touches Fejos on his arm...

216 MED. SHOT

Before Fejos realizes what is happening, Daniel rushes in, snatches the whip from the Gipsy's hand and lashes him across the face.

CONTINUED

216   CONTINUED

Fejos and Urla throw themselves upon the hunchback. Daniel flings the woman aside, closes his hands about Fejos' throat and starts choking him just as Niemann appears, in background...

217   CLOSE SHOT - NIEMANN

As he sees what is happening, he runs in a PAN SHOT toward the Gipsies' wagon...

218   MED. SHOT

Daniel's fingers lock tighter and tighter about Fejos' throat. Urla, fighting him like a wild woman, is trying to drag Daniel away from her man as Niemann reaches the pair and grabs Daniel's wrists.

           NIEMANN
     Do you want the Police on us, you fool!?
          (to Fejos, as he flings
           Daniel off)
     Get out -- before he kills you!

The Gipsies run toward their wagon as Daniel, grabbing the whip from the ground, cuts its lash across Fejos' back in one last moment of blind fury -- following which, he runs in a PAN SHOT to where Ilonka still lies motionless....

219   CLOSE SHOT - ILONKA AND DANIEL

As Daniel looks down at the girl, his fury of a moment ago is replaced by an expression in which there is something akin to worshipful awe. He lifts her tenderly in his arms and stands to his feet as Niemann enters.

           DANIEL
     Master....She's hurt....May I take her
     with us?

           NIEMANN
     If it'll keep you in your right senses!
          (as Daniel's face lights up)
     Finish packing. We have until morning
     to search for the Frankenstein records -
     and we can't waste time...

Almost as though he hadn't heard Niemann, Daniel is carrying Ilonka toward the van as the scene

                                        DISSOLVES INTO

220   EXT. LAMPINI CARAVAN - CAMPFIRE - CLOSE SHOT

Steam is hissing from the spout of a battered brass kettle which rests upon the rocks of a campfire. A hand is lifting the kettle and pouring its brew into a cup as the CAMERA PULLS BACK into a LARGER SHOT, revealing Daniel.

As he leaves the campfire, the CAMERA PANS with him, the CHANGING ANGLE showing his progress past the Lampini living-wagon, whose windows are bright from the light within.

221   MED. CLOSE SHOT - FRONT OF VAN

A lantern hangs upon a hook on the side of the wagon. Daniel enters and climbs up into the driver's seat.

222   INT. VAN - DRIVER'S SEAT - FULL SHOT

Back of the seat is a small compartment in which is a narrow bunk. The light from the lantern illuminates only one side of this cubby. Lying in the bunk is Ilonka, asleep. Daniel puts the cup on a shelf, swings his legs over the driver's seat and sits on a three-legged stool beside the bunk, in the semi-darkness. He bends over into the light, so that he can look down into Ilonka's face. Illuminated by the soft lantern light, Ilonka presents a pretty picture.

223   CLOSE SHOT - DANIEL

Ilonka's beauty brings a moment of warped tenderness into the hunchback's hardened face.

224   FULL SHOT

As Daniel moves the stool to reach for the cup, the noise disturbs Ilonka. As she turns, Daniel draws back into the darkness. He speaks almost in a whisper.

                    DANIEL
          Are you awake...?

Ilonka opens her eyes - then suddenly sits upright and starts pummeling the dimly seen figure. Daniel grasps her arms and gently forces her back onto the bunk.

                    DANIEL
          You've nothing to be afraid of, now....

                                        CONTINUED

224   CONTINUED

Ilonka relaxes, weak from exertion. Daniel leans back into the darkness. Ilonka's voice is contrite.

> ILONKA
> I - I must have been - dreaming...
> (trying to see him)
> Who are you?

> DANIEL
> I'm Daniel.... I'm with Professor Lampini's show.
> (taking the cup)
> Here's some tea. It'll make you feel better ---

Ilonka sits up. Still obscured from her view, Daniel offers her the cup. Ilonka takes it, gratefully.

> ILONKA
> That's nice of you, Daniel...
> (after a sip)
> Are you the one who helped me?

> DANIEL
> (remembering, angrily)
> It made me mad when he whipped you...
> He can't hurt you again. They've gone...

> ILONKA
> (a little laugh)
> Leaving me a hundred miles from nowhere...

> DANIEL
> We're going to Visaria -- Doctor Niemann said you can travel with us...

> ILONKA
> That would be wonderful!

> DANIEL
> You can sleep here --
> (almost pleading)
> -- and talk to me sometimes, when I drive...
> I'm lonesome, at night - with no one to talk to...

> ILONKA
> I'll talk you to death!

> DANIEL
> (as she sips her tea)
> Your name's Ilonka, isn't it?

CONTINUED

224 CONTINUED - 2

                    ILONKA
          You know all about me, don't you?

                    DANIEL
          I watched you dance...

                    ILONKA
          Did you, Daniel? Did you like me?

                    DANIEL
                    (very quietly)
          You're pretty...

                    ILONKA
                    (teasingly)
          You're afraid of me, aren't you?

                    DANIEL
          Afraid of you...?

                    ILONKA
                    (flirtatiously)
          If you weren't you'd sit over here -
          where I could see you...

There is a pause. Then, Daniel leans forward so that his face and figure come slowly into the light.

Ilonka draws back with an involuntary reaction of revulsion as she sees his ugly face and deformed body.

                    ILONKA
          Oh! You're...
                    (stops quickly)

                    DANIEL
          An ugly hunchback...
                    (like a little child)
          But you'll talk to me, sometimes, won't you?

Ilonka rests her hand upon his in a gesture of impulsive contrite sympathy.

                    ILONKA
          Of course, I will! You've been kind
          to me -- and I like you...

He looks at her in worshipful silence, interrupted by the sounds of sharp knocking on the side of the van.

                    DANIEL
          Yes, Master?

p1

225   EXT. FRONT OF VAN - MED. CLOSE SHOT

Niemann, carrying a hooded lantern, is waiting.

             NIEMANN
     Bring your lantern....Hurry.

226   INT. VAN COMPARTMENT - FULL SHOT

Daniel gets to his feet and takes the lantern, turning its hood so that the light is almost obscured.

             DANIEL
          (to Ilonka, assuringly)
     Go to sleep and rest -- I'll be back
     in a little while...

He starts to climb over the seat.

227   EXT. FRONT OF VAN - MED. CLOSE SHOT

As Daniel climbs down and joins Niemann, the two of them move off into the darkness as the scene

                              DISSOLVES INTO

228   EXT. FRANKENSTEIN RUINS - MED. FULL SHOT

The scene is one of desolation -- a rock-strewn path up which Daniel and Niemann are laboriously climbing.

As they come through foreground and the CAMERA PANS WITH THEM, a portion of the Frankenstein ruins are brought into view -- a few broken walls and some tumbled down masonry, over which Daniel leads the way as the scene

                              WIPES INTO

229   INT. FRANKENSTEIN LABORATORY - MED. CLOSE - STAIRS

A diffused glow of light from their lanterns reveals the stone stairs, down which clatters a small piece of masonry, from above. As the noise breaks the silence, bats take off into the night with frightened squeaks.

Niemann appears, followed by Daniel. As they descend the rubble-strewn stairs, the CAMERA PULLS BACK into a LARGER SHOT which shows what was once Frankenstein's laboratory - a roofless, barren room whose masonry-strewn floor is covered with a layer of dried silt, left there by the waters which swept through it, years ago.

                              CONTINUED

229   CONTINUED

A twisted steel operating table lies across a large, circular opening in the floor. Coming up to the edge of this opening from the room below, is an iron ladder.

230   CLOSE SHOT - DANIEL AND NIEMANN

As they turn their lanterns in various directions, the CAMERA MOVES AHEAD OF THEM until the circular opening is in MEDIUM FOREGROUND.

Niemann shoves the table out of the way, directs the beam of his lantern into the space below - then starts down the ladder. Daniel waits a moment, then follows....

231   INT. BASEMENT ROOM - MED. CLOSE - FOOT OF LADDER

The ladder is on the right. Niemann is on the bottom rung and Daniel is following him down as the CAMERA ANGLES AROUND into a LARGER SHOT.

The floor of this room is also covered by a layer of dried, cracked silt. Spider webs stretch across the corners.

Daniel joins Niemann. Together, they sweep the bare room with their lanterns - which reveal a large gap, torn in the upscene masonry wall. Across the bottom of this gap, pinioned there by the force of the outrushing flood, is a rusty metal cage, of the size and shape to accommodate a large, human body. Held in its twisted mesh, are pieces of smaller apparatus of nondescript size and nature.

The CAMERA FOLLOWS Niemann and Daniel as they move toward these objects - which Niemann examines in the closer light of his lantern and then throws aside, with reactions of disappointment.

When the last of these props has been removed, Niemann raises his lantern and directs its beam into the opening.

          NIEMANN
     The force of the flood broke through
     this wall and sucked everything into
     the cave, beyond...We must search for
     the records I need, in there...

Daniel raises his lantern so that both his and Niemann's faces are in full illumination. There is new and keener intensity in the hunchback's voice.

          DANIEL
     And if we find them, will you make me
     - like other men?

                              CONTINUED

31   CONTINUED

                    NIEMANN
          To please your little Gipsy girl?
               (amused)
          Yes, friend Daniel -- I will make
          you an Adonis...

     He drags the cage away from the entrance, unaware of the
     resentment his amusement has brought into Daniel's eyes.

     When the opening is free, Niemann sweeps away a veil of
     spider-webs and steps through into

32   INT. PASSAGE - MED. CLOSE SHOT

     As Niemann and Daniel step through the opening the CAMERA
     MOVES AHEAD OF THEM, revealing a natural gallery in the
     limestone rock. Its floor has been swept clean by the
     torrent which rushed through it years before, and its
     sweating walls glisten in the light from the lanterns.

                    DANIEL
          Master -- it's cold...

                    NIEMANN
          It comes from the glacial ice, below...

     As they continue onward, the scene

                                        WIPES INTO

33   INT. PASSAGE - ANOTHER SET UP - MED. CLOSE SHOT

     Moving ahead of Niemann and Daniel, the CAMERA now brings
     them into a section of the passage upon whose ice-incrusted
     walls the seep-water trickles in glistening streams which
     reflect and multiply the light from the lantern.

     Here and there, a few objects from the laboratory have
     lodged in crevices - pieces of broken apparatus, parts of
     wooden laboratory furniture, a twisted metal chair, etc.

     Moving slower than before, Niemann's eyes shift from
     object to object, hoping to see some evidence of the
     records he seeks. Daniel, behind him, does likewise.

                                        WIPE INTO

34   INT. PASSAGE TO ICE CAVE - MED. CLOSE SHOT

     The slope of the passage becomes steeper as the CAMERA
     MOVES AHEAD of Niemann and Daniel.

                                        CONTINUED

234   CONTINUED

Niemann sees a piece of paper, caught in a fissure. He snatches at it hopefully - but throws it aside after inspecting it in the light of his lantern.

As the MOVEMENT continues, the passage makes a turn and widens out.

Niemann, held by what he sees ahead, stops in the mouth of the passage while the CAMERA MOVES AWAY and ANGLES AROUND IN 90 DEGREES to show a large cavern - a place of ice-incrusted stalactites and stalagmites whose fantastic shapes glisten in the lanterns' light.

Opposite the passage, there is a niche. In this lies the body of the Monster, encased in ice some eight or ten inches thick, but which still outlines his enormous form.

Slightly downscene from this niche is a natural opening in the wall - a hole about three feet in diameter, against which a heterogeneous assortment of wooden laboratory furniture and scientific apparatus has been lodged by the outrush of the flood-water.

Near this, leaning against the wall and frozen there in a distorted position, is another ice-incrusted body - that of the Wolf Man.

As Niemann and Daniel cross the cavern, the CAMERA PANS AND MOVES UP WITH THEM until they stop near the Wolf Man. Here, Niemann raises his lantern higher and holds it closer to the ice-incrusted figure.

235   CLOSE SHOT - WOLF MAN

Glacial seepage drips upon the figure, leaving the ice crystal clear. Through it is seen the Wolf Man's face, on which is a weird, hirsute growth. His eyes are closed. One hairy hand is near his mouth - as if, in his final struggle, he had sought to fight away the engulfing waters.

236   CLOSE SHOT - NIEMANN AND DANIEL

Daniel, shivering in the icy air, is awed by what he sees.

                    NIEMANN
    The Wolf Man...

The CAMERA MOVES WITH HIM AND DANIEL, until they stop before the niche in which lies the Monster. Here, also, the glacial seepage has polished the ice into clearness so that the Monster's form is clearly seen.

                              CONTINUED

36   CONTINUED

Niemann steps closer so that he can look down at --

37   CLOSE SHOT - MONSTER

His eyes are closed. Upon the grotesque face there is an expression almost of peace - as though, in this icy prison, the Monster had found surcease from misery.

38   CLOSE SHOT - NIEMANN AND DANIEL

Niemann's eyes light up with the elation of a scientist, as:

>   NIEMANN
>   The undying Monster --- the triumphant
>   climax of Frankenstein's genius...
>   (looking off)
>   And the Wolf Man...
>   (to Daniel)
>   They may know where the records are,
>   friend Daniel...We will set them free -
>   and they will help us...

Daniel's teeth chatter from fear and from the breath of this icy tomb.

>   DANIEL
>   M-M-Master....We'll freeze....

Niemann is holding his lantern closer to look at the Monster's face again as the scene

                                          DISSOLVES INTO

39   CLOSE SHOT - FIRE

Pieces of the broken laboratory furniture are blazing in a large pile. Offscene, are heard sounds of Niemann and Daniel, working to free the Monster from the ice.

As the CAMERA LEAVES THE FIRE AND MOVES UP into a CLOSE SHOT, we see that the heat has begun to melt the ice and that one of the Wolf Man's hairy hands is now free. The muscles of the fingers begin to work as the CAMERA SWINGS AROUND to show Niemann and Daniel, chopping the ice from the Monster's body with tools improvised from the metal apparatus.

Again, the CAMERA ANGLES to the Wolf Man, coming to a stop in a MEDIUM CLOSE SHOT in which the melting process is completed by a series of PROGRESSIVE DISSOLVES.

                                          CONTINUED

239   CONTINUED

When the last of the ice has disappeared, ANOTHER DISSOLVE removes the hairy growth from the Wolf Man's face and hands and transmutes him into a human being, LARRY TALBOT, whose eyes open slowly and stare off toward --

240   CLOSE SHOT - NIEMANN AND DANIEL

Unaware of the change that has taken place in the Wolf Man, Niemann and Daniel continue their work.

241   CLOSE SHOT - LARRY

The realization that he has been brought back to a world of misery, brings dark anger and despair into Larry's eyes. As he gets to his feet, he picks up a piece of heavy metal and moves toward Niemann and Daniel in a PAN SHOT which brings them into view.

> LARRY
> Who are you!?

Niemann and Daniel whirl. As Larry raises his weapon threateningly, Daniel shrinks closer to Niemann, in awed fear.

> LARRY (continuing)
> Why have you freed me from the ice which for all these years has imprisoned the werewolf which lives within me?
> (advancing menacingly)
> Why? Why!?

> NIEMANN
> (craftily)
> To help you, perhaps...

> LARRY
> No earthly power can help those who are marked by the sign of the beast!

His speech becomes an emotional torrent in which he lays bare his broken hopes and the tragedy of his being.

> LARRY (continued)
> When I found that I had become a victim of the werewolf's curse, I escaped from a hospital in England and came here, thinking that Doctor Frankenstein could help me...
> (torn by the memory)
> But he was dead! -- Hope for the release

CONTINUED

241 CONTINUED

>   LARRY (continued)
>   I sought died, too -- until Doctor
>   Mannering, who followed my trail of
>   death across Europe, persuaded
>   Frankenstein's daughter to give him
>   her father's records - so that by
>   means of his secrets, the forces of
>   the eternal life to which I am doomed,
>   might be drained away...
>
>   NIEMANN
>   (eagerly)
>   Did Mannering try the experiment?
>
>   LARRY
>   The villagers learned that he was
>   bringing the Monster back to life...
>   They blew up the dam, whose frozen
>   waters imprisoned me, here...
>   (raising his weapon)
>   And now you have brought me back to
>   a world of misery! When the moon is
>   full, I turn into a wolf! I kill people!
>   (breaking suddenly)
>   I want to die! Only death can bring
>   release...

He drops his weapon and covers his face with his hands.

>   NIEMANN
>   You are wrong. I am a doctor, a
>   scientist...I say --

242 CLOSE SHOT - NIEMANN AND LARRY

>   NIEMANN (continued)
>   -- there is no need for you to die...
>   I can help you...
>
>   LARRY
>   How? How can you help me?
>
>   NIEMANN
>   Do you know where Frankenstein's
>   records are?
>
>   LARRY
>   (closing his eyes, trying to
>   remember)
>   I...I think so...
>
>   NIEMANN
>   Show me where they are - and I will
>   build you a new brain. I will remove
>   the curse from you, forever...

CONTINUED

242   CONTINUED

>   LARRY
>   His diary was hidden in the laboratory...

                                        DISSOLVE INTO

243   INT. FRANKENSTEIN RUINS - CLOSEUP - WALL

Light from an offscene lantern shows Larry's hand, pressing against one end of a stone block. This turns on a pivot, disclosing that its thickness is only about two inches. On the side which swings into view is a small shelf, hollowed out in the form of a drawer. In this lies the Frankenstein Diary - a leather-bound book upon the cover of which is the old style lettering:

                    EXPERIMENTS
                         in
                    Life and Death

                    Henry Frankenstein

As Larry's hand removes the diary and two or three other cloth-bound books which lie beneath it, the scene

                                        DISSOLVES INTO

244   INT. LAMPINI LIVING-WAGON - FULL SHOT - NIGHT

The view is a FOREGROUND SHOT across the bunk in which lies the Monster, inert, hands crossed upon his chest.

On the seat beneath the windows, is Larry. His bowed head rests upon the upturned palms of his hands.

Niemann has pushed one of the Monster's eyelids back and is leaning over, to make an examination. Frowning dubiously, he steps to the fold-down table, upon which a small pot of water is steaming over an oil burner. He dips a folded towel into the water and wrings it out, following which he wraps the compress around the exposed lower half of one of the Monster's scarred arms. Larry looks up.

>   LARRY
>   Is he dead...?
>
>   NIEMANN
>   Frankenstein's creation is immortal...
>   In my laboratory at Visaria, I have
>   apparatus which will restore his strength...

                                        CONTINUED

244 CONTINUED

Larry springs to his feet in resentment.

              LARRY
Must I wait and suffer - and take the lives of innocent people while you try to bring that inhuman Monster back to life!? Why must you do *that*, first? You said you could cure *me*! Do it, then!
        (picking up Frankenstein's
         diary)
All you need is here!
        (he buries his face in his
         hands)
Help me! Help me, before the moon is full again!

             NIEMANN
        (resting a hand upon
         Larry's shoulder)
Patience, my boy. It is true that I have Frankenstein's records -- but the road ahead is dark -- and difficult...

The door of the wagon opens and Daniel steps inside.

             DANIEL
The horses are harnessed, Master...

             NIEMANN
        (to Larry)
Can you drive?

             LARRY
        (dully)
Yes...

             NIEMANN
Take the road to Visaria..
        (to Daniel)
Stay here. I want you to help me.

Daniel, knowing that Larry will be with Ilonka, looks after him with sudden jealousy as the scene

                    DISSOLVES INTO

245 EXT. CLOSE SHOT - WHEELS OF VAN - <u>NIGHT</u>

Offscene, are heard noises of the restless horses, followed by a crack of a whip which starts them off and sets the wheels into motion with a sudden jerk.

246   INT. VAN COMPARTMENT - FULL SHOT - NIGHT

The sudden start awakens Ilonka and almost rolls her out of the bunk. Seeing the silhouetted figure in front of her and assuming that it is Daniel, she climbs quietly up beside him.

247   INT. DRIVER'S SEAT OF VAN - MED. CLOSE SHOT

Larry is staring into the night as Ilonka swings herself around on the seat, gaily.

                    ILONKA
          Hello, Daniel!

Larry turns in surprise. Ilonka is wordless as she sees that he isn't Daniel, but someone who more nearly fulfills her idea of what a hero should look like.

                    LARRY
          Daniel's with Doctor Niemann...

                    ILONKA
               (provocatively)
          Who're you?

                    LARRY
               (looking ahead, again)
          Lawrence Talbot.

                    ILONKA
          Are you going to Visaria, with us?

                    LARRY
          Yes.

Ilonka leans forward in an effort to see Larry better. When he remains unconscious of her interest, she makes a little moue, of pique.

                    ILONKA
          I promised Daniel I'd keep him company
          while he drove -- but I'll talk to you --
          if you want me to...

                    LARRY
          I don't want to talk.

                    ILONKA
          Not even a little bit?

                    LARRY
               (in sudden anger)
          Leave me alone, will you?

                                        CONTINUED

47   CONTINUED

                    ILONKA
          All right --
                    (flirtatiously)
          -- Larry.

     She swings herself around and drops down into the
     compartment.

48   INT. VAN COMPARTMENT - MED. CLOSE SHOT

     Ilonka, smiling happily, falls back into the bunk, prop-
     ping the pillow under her head so that she can look up
     toward the silhouetted figure of Larry as the scene

                                              DISSOLVES INTO

49   EXT. COUNTRYSIDE - ROADSIGN - CLOSE SHOT - <u>DAY</u>

     An arrow pointing to the left is below the legend:

                    VISARIA - 107 km.

     The CAMERA ANGLES to the caravan, which has stopped for
     a rest among the trees a little distance from the road.

                                              DISSOLVE TO

50   MED. FOREGROUND SHOT - OVER CAMPFIRE

     No one is in sight but Daniel, coming toward the campfire
     from the living-wagon. He starts to lift the bucket of
     water which is heating upon the stones, but pauses and
     looks off as he hears:

                    ILONKA'S VOICE
               (offscene, calling gaily)
          Larry! Larry!

51   A NEARBY BROOK - MED. CLOSE SHOT - ILONKA

     She has been wading, and is picked up in action as she
     runs toward shore.

                    ILONKA (continued)
          Wait for me...!

     The CAMERA ANGLES and picks up Larry, a little distance
     upscene, walking among the trees as Ilonka runs after him.

52 CAMPFIRE - DANIEL - CLOSE SHOT

Jealous anger comes into his eyes as he stands there, watching....

53 AMONG TREES - MOVING SHOT - MED. CLOSE

The CAMERA IS MOVING ahead of Larry as Ilonka catches up with him, breathless.

Larry's thoughts are gloomy and far away. Ilonka is flirtatious.

> ILONKA
> We've been together three days, now -- and you've hardly looked at me!

Larry remains silent. Ilonka is piqued.

> ILONKA
> I think I'd like you -- if you smiled.
> (as Larry turns to her, angrily)
> Now don't start barking!
> (beaming)
> There's a nice big smile for you!
> Now you give *me* one!

Her winsome charm breaks Larry down. In spite of himself, a smile comes over his face. Ilonka is gaily triumphant.

> ILONKA
> You see how easy it is!

Taking his arm, she tugs him toward a fallen tree.

54 CAMPFIRE - CLOSE SHOT - DANIEL

Smoldering jealousy is in his eyes as he looks off toward--

55 FALLEN TREE - CLOSE SHOT - LARRY AND ILONKA

They sit down. Larry, lapsing into his former mood, picks up a twig and starts making marks upon the ground.

Ilonka, sensing that he carries some troubling secret, becomes more serious.

> ILONKA
> Why are you always so sad...?
> (reacting to Larry's deepening frown)
> I wish you'd tell me,...

CONTINUED

255 CONTINUED

>   LARRY
>   (without looking at her)
>   Why?
>
>   ILONKA
>   Because I like you.

She edges closer. Larry turns to her as if on the verge of unburdening himself.

>   ILONKA
>   (seeing his hesitation)
>   Tell me....
>
>   LARRY
>   Do you see what I've drawn?

Ilonka, puzzled, looks down at --

256 CLOSEUP - GROUND NEAR LARRY'S FEET

There are some meaningless marks, but in prominence among them is a five-pointed star.

>   ILONKA'S VOICE
>   It's a five-pointed star --

257 CLOSE SHOT - ILONKA AND LARRY

Sudden shock comes into Ilonka's voice as she looks up at him with realization of the star's significance.

>   ILONKA (continued)
>   -- the pentagram!
>
>   LARRY
>   "Even a man who is pure at heart,
>   And says his prayers by night -
>   May become a wolf, when the wolfbane blooms,
>   And the moon is full and bright."

With an intensity of emotion which floods his face with misery, Larry tears open his shirt front, exposing the scar upon his chest - the pentagram.

>   LARRY
>   The mark of the beast -- made by the
>   werewolf who attacked me....

He turns his eyes from hers. Ilonka, shocked by what he has revealed, draws away....

258   CAMPFIRE - CLOSE SHOT - DANIEL

Daniel enjoys a moment of satisfaction as he sees Ilonka's reaction...

259   FALLEN TREE - CLOSE SHOT - LARRY AND ILONKA

Recovering from her shock, Ilonka edges closer to Larry. Her voice is softly sympathetic.

> ILONKA
> Larry...I -- I'm not afraid...
>
> LARRY
> You will be -- when the full moon shines.
>
> ILONKA
> No! I won't! I'll try to help you!

She rests her hand on his arm...

260   CAMPFIRE - CLOSE SHOT - DANIEL

Ilonka's sympathy adds fuel to Daniel's jealousy...

261   FALLEN TREE - CLOSE SHOT - LARRY AND ILONKA

Larry is looking straight ahead of him, as though into the darkness of his uncertain future.

> LARRY
> Doctor Niemann says he can perform a brain operation which will -- cure me.
>
> ILONKA
> Will he do it soon...?
>
> LARRY
> He says that first he must restore the Monster's vitality - so that he can study Frankenstein's technique...
>   (besieged)
> But he must do it before the full moon comes again! He must, he must!

Ilonka rests her head upon Larry's shoulder and her hand upon his arm. Her voice is soft.

> ILONKA
> Poor Larry...

Larry is touched by Ilonka's evident sincerity and affection. He smiles at her as they rise and start slowly in the direction of the caravan....

262 END OF LIVING-WAGON - MED. CLOSE - NIEMANN

He comes down the steps to the ground, looking off toward the campfire with a flash of anger.

> NIEMANN
> Hurry with that water! Are you going to stand there, all day...!?

263 CAMPFIRE - MED. SHOT - DANIEL

With a last jealous look toward Larry and Ilonka, who are appearing in background, Daniel takes the bucket and starts toward the living-wagon...

264 END OF LIVING-WAGON - MED. CLOSE - NIEMANN

He looks off, frowning as he sees....

265 ILONKA AND LARRY - MED. SHOT

They are walking slowly toward the caravan...

266 END OF LIVING-WAGON - MED. CLOSE - NIEMANN

There is irritation in his voice as he calls:

> NIEMANN
> Get started! We've lost too much time as it is!

Daniel enters, carrying the bucket of water. He meets Niemann's angry eyes with a surly glance - then enters the living-wagon. Niemann glances off toward Ilonka and Larry, then follows Daniel in --

267 LAMPINI CARAVAN - MED. SHOT

Larry and Ilonka are hurrying toward the van...

268 INT. LAMPINI LIVING-WAGON - FULL SHOT

ANGLE ACROSS THE MONSTER, ON THE BUNK, beside which sits Niemann. As Daniel wrings out a towel which he has dipped in the hot water, Niemann unwinds a similar compress from one of the Monster's exposed arms...

269 CLOSE SHOT - NIEMANN

He lifts the Monster's scarred arm and tries to dent the hardened flesh with his finger-nail. Examining the result with disappointment, Niemann bends the arm back into position upon the Monster's chest.

CONTINUED

269   CONTINUED

                    NIEMANN
          Dessication of the tissues has gone
          farther than I thought...
                    (as he rises)
          Keep at it...

Daniel wraps the fresh compress about the Monster's arm.

270   FULL SHOT

A jolt, accompanied by offscene creaking of the wagon's wheels, indicates that the caravan is under way. Niemann sits in Lampini's rocking-chair and picks up Frankenstein's Diary, lying open on the nearby shelf...

                    DANIEL
          Master...
                    (turning toward Niemann)
          Is the Wolf Man going to drive all
          the time?

                    NIEMANN
          Yes...He bothers me with his ever-
          lasting questions ---
                    (finding his place in
                    the diary)
          My chief concern is to get the Monster
          to Visaria, before further changes
          make restoration more difficult...

He becomes engrossed in the diary. Daniel gives him a surly look - then resumes business with the compress as the scene

                                        DISSOLVES INTO

271   EXT. ROADSIGN - CLOSE SHOT - NIGHT

The CAMERA SWINGS on the sign:

                    VISARIA - 1 km.

                                        DISSOLVE INTO

272   EXT. NEAR GATES TO NIEMANN'S ESTATE - FULL SHOT - NIGHT

The CAMERA PANS with the caravan as its wheels groan over a disused road, rank with an overgrowth of weeds. A high, masonry wall comes into view. Set in this are huge iron gates, so thickly covered with ivy that they seem almost a part of the wall itself.

As the caravan stops, Niemann and Daniel appear from the living-wagon and hurry toward the gates, followed by Larry, who climbs down from the driver's seat of the van. Niemann carries an iron bar.

273   MED. CLOSE SHOT - NEAR GATES

   Following Niemann's silent lead, Daniel and Larry assist in tearing the ivy away, so that the gates begin to show.

274   INT. DRIVER'S SEAT OF VAN - ILONKA - CLOSE SHOT

   She is looking off toward the action at the gates.

275   EXT. GATES TO NIEMANN'S ESTATE - MED. CLOSE SHOT

   As Niemann tears away the ivy near the middle part of the gates, a wooden sign is brought into view.

276   CLOSE SHOT - SIGN

   It is bolted to the metal bars, near a rusty iron chain which is padlocked around the framework of the gates. The almost obliterated legend on the weather-beaten board reads:

   > Entrance to These Grounds
   > FORBIDDEN
   > Gustav Niemann

   Niemann's hands enter the picture with the iron bar, putting it through the loop of the chain and twisting it so that the bar will act as a lever.

277   MED. SHOT

   When the chain fails to give way, Larry adds his grip to the bar. The chain breaks.

   Niemann, Daniel and Larry now throw their weights against the gates. They creak slowly open.

278   INT. DRIVER'S SEAT OF VAN - CLOSE SHOT - ILONKA

   As she hears the gates creaking open, Ilonka takes up the reins and slaps them over the horses' flanks.

279   MED. FULL SHOT

   The caravan passes through the gates. As the vehicles disappear, the gates are being closed from inside the grounds as the scene

   DISSOLVES INTO

280   INT. NIEMANN'S LABORATORY - NEAR STAIR BALCONY - NIGHT

The CAMERA PULLS BACK, showing Niemann and Ilonka as they appear around the turn of a corridor. This terminates on a low, railed platform, from which two broad steps lead down into the laboratory. Niemann carries the Frankenstein Diary and other books under one arm.

Ilonka, awesomely impressed, follows Niemann's example as he holds his lantern higher, to light the way for Larry and Daniel, behind them. They come into view, carrying the Monster, whose body is covered by a blanket.

As the CAMERA CONTINUES TO PULL BACK, the WIDENING ANGLE brings other portions of the laboratory into view. Apparently in an old castle, the architecture reflects this character.

At the far end is an alcove, in which is set a tremendously large, glazed window on both sides of which hang heavy drapes, festooned with cob-webs of the passing years.

We see now that the laboratory duplicates the picture drawn by Niemann on the wall of his dungeon. In foreground are the laboratory tables and switchboard, with the high-frequency apparatus, nearby. Veils of cob-webs stretch over everything.

Niemann sweeps the cob-webs from one of the operating tables as Larry and Daniel approach.

                    NIEMANN
          Put him here...

Larry and Daniel put the Monster's body on the table, Niemann starts toward the window. Ilonka, obviously uninformed as to what lies under the blanket, steps closer to Larry. She speaks in a hushed whisper.

                    ILONKA
          What is it?

                    DANIEL
                (quickly)
          The Frankenstein Monster!

He draws back the blanket, exposing the Monster's face. Ilonka turns away with a frightened gasp and buries her face against Larry's chest.

Daniel, seeing that his bit of exhititionism has lost him the spotlight he expected, scowls jealously.

281 MED. SHOT - NEAR LARGE WINDOW

Niemann is pulling the drapes closed, stretching the cob-webs into sticky threads which lace themselves across the velvet in fantastic patterns.

The CAMERA ANGLES as Niemann moves to a part of the wall on which hangs an ancient, metal shield. He swings this aside, revealing a small wall safe. Opening this, Niemann removes a securities box and takes out some of the money it contains.

282 GROUP SHOT - ANGLING OVER THE MONSTER'S TABLE

Ilonka, still clinging to Larry's arm, is staring with frightened eyes at the Monster as Niemann comes down-scene.

                  NIEMANN
            (handing Larry the money)
You and the girl go into the village and purchase supplies....Answer no questions as to who you are, or where you are staying...No one must know I've returned to Visaria...

283 CLOSE SHOT - DANIEL

Jealousy seizes him as his eyes follow Larry and Ilonka.

284 MED. SHOT - TOWARD STAIR LANDING

As seen from Daniel's angle, Larry and Ilonka are nearing the landing. Ilonka is clinging to Larry's arm.

285 CLOSE SHOT - DANIEL

As OFFSCENE SOUNDS indicate that Ilonka and Larry have exited, Daniel moves in a PAN SHOT to Niemann. He is looking down into the Monster's face.

                  DANIEL
Master...
            (as Niemann looks up)
She likes the Wolf Man --
            (purring)
Will you give me his body -- so that she'll like me, instead?

                  NIEMANN
I have other plans for the Wolf Man...

CONTINUED

285 CONTINUED

> DANIEL
> You made me a promise.
>
> NIEMANN
> All in good time -- after you've helped me even the score with the others who sent me to prison...

286 CLOSE SHOT - NIEMANN

His eyes gleam and his voice becomes harsh and bitter.

> NIEMANN (continued)
> To Ullman, my old assistant --
>   (looking down into
>   the Monster's face)
> I'll give the Monster's worn-out body - a fitting gift to repay him for betraying me...
>   (smiling sarcastically
>   at Daniel, who steps
>   into view)
> As for Strauss, the talkative gentleman who saw me in the graveyard -- I'll give him the brain of the Wolf Man, so that he will become a werewolf...
>
> DANIEL
> And give me the Wolf Man's body!?
>
> NIEMANN
> No. Talbot's body is young, and strong - a proper place for the Monster's brain - which I will add to and subtract from, in my experiments to create the perfect man...
>   (he picks up the Diary and
>   other books)
> Start straightening up in here --

The CAMERA ANGLES to show his progress toward a door, in the wall opposite the stair landing.

287 CLOSE SHOT - DANIEL

He looks after Niemann with anger and then, when OFFSCENE SOUNDS indicate that Niemann has left the room, steps closer to the table. Here, holding high the lantern left by Larry and Ilonka, he looks down at --

288   DOWNWARD ANGLE - ON MONSTER'S FACE

Daniel bends into the picture. There is dark hatred in his face as he snarls at the apparently lifeless figure.

> DANIEL
> So he's going to give <u>you</u> the Wolf Man's body!

He climaxes his rage by spitting at the Monster's face as the SCENE

> DISSOLVE INTO

289   INSERT - CLOSEUP - FRANKENSTEIN DIARY

Niemann's hand opens the book to a page on which is a sketch showing a glass case covering the body of the Monster, which lies on an operating table. From this case, a flexible hose leads to an autoclave - a steam-generating piece of apparatus.

> DISSOLVE INTO

290   INT. NIEMANN'S LABORATORY - MED. SHOT - <u>NIGHT</u>

Since last seen, the laboratory has been made spotless. The illumination is from a large overhead lamp, similar to those used in modern operating rooms.

The setup duplicates the perspectives of the drawing, so that the effect is that of changing the drawing into reality. The Monster lies on one of the operating tables, covered by a glass case. Above it is a block and tackle, with wires hooked onto all four corners, so that the case may be raised or lowered.

Niemann is completing the connection of the steam line from the autoclave. Larry stands nearby, watching with deep interest behind which is desperate hope.

> NIEMANN
> (to Daniel)
> Turn on the steam...

291   MED. CLOSE SHOT - AUTOCLAVE

Daniel turns the valve. The sound of steam passing through the pipe is heard. As the CAMERA PANS to the Monster's table, steam jets through the opening and begins to fill the case.

292   MED. CLOSE SHOT - NIEMANN AND LARRY

Niemann observes the effect with satisfaction.

>   NIEMANN
> The steam will soften the tissues --
> so that the high-frequency currents
> can pass through them...

>   LARRY
> How long will it take?

>   NIEMANN
>   (shrugs)
> A day -- perhaps longer.

>   LARRY
> The full moon will rise at midnight!
>   (desperately)
> Operate on me now! I can't --
>   (closing his eyes)
> -- go through that horror, again!
> I can't!

>   NIEMANN
> To operate before discovering a
> method of combining Frankenstein's
> technique with my own would leave
> you as you are. You must wait.

>   LARRY
> Wait, wait, wait...!

He turns from the table. Niemann looks after him without emotion as Larry crosses the room in a PAN SHOT and EXITS through the door on the right, into --

293   INT. HALL IN NIEMANN'S CASTLE - FULL SHOT - NIGHT

Larry ENTERS and crosses blindly toward the door of his room, opposite....

294   INT. LARRY'S ROOM - MED. CLOSE AT DOOR

Larry ENTERS, closing the door. He stands there for a moment, examining his hands, back and front - as though in terror of discovering evidences of the hirsute growth which comes when he changes into the Wolf Man. Then, with a choked sob, he runs across the room in a FAST PAN SHOT toward the French doors which open into the garden.

295   EXT. NIEMANN'S GARDEN - FRENCH DOORS TO LARRY'S ROOM - MED. CLOSE SHOT - NIGHT

After years of neglect, the shrubbery is rank and overgrown and the pathways are filled with weeds.

As Larry ENTERS, the CAMERA PICKS HIM UP IN A PAN SHOT, following him as he runs toward a solid wooden gate set in the stone wall UPSCENE. Larry flings the gate open and is exiting as the SCENE

DISSOLVES INTO

296   EXT. FOREST - LONG SHOT - NIGHT

In a PAN SHOT, Larry is in headlong flight, as though trying to run away from the horror which will soon be upon him.

297   CLOSE SHOT - LARRY

He runs into a CLOSE SHOT, stopping in emotional frenzy as he looks toward --

298   EXT. HORIZON - LONG SHOT - (STOCK) - NIGHT

The clouds are parting. The full moon begins to show --

299   CLOSE SHOT - LARRY

As the moonlight falls upon his face, Larry looks frantically at his hands. Then, covering his face, he runs off into the night as the CAMERA PANS UP, showing the full moon, clear and brilliant in an open patch of sky.

Hold on this for several seconds. Then, as the chilling howl of the werewolf comes through the night,

DISSOLVE INTO

300   EXT. VISARIA STREET - MED. FULL SHOT - NIGHT

A little distance UPSCENE, a criss-crossed pattern of lights and shadows fall into the street, cast by lamps from within a small tavern, on a corner. It is toward the windows of the tavern that the CAMERA IS MOVING as the SCENE

DISSOLVES INTO

301   ANGLING THROUGH TAVERN WINDOW, FROM EXTERIOR - MED. CLOSE

Seated at a table near the window are three villagers. All are of different types and are on the better side of forty. Three steins of beer are in evidence. Two of the men are playing checkers.

The third man is STRAUSS, "the talkative gentleman who saw Niemann in the graveyard." He is a gravedigger type, a man in his middle fifties. Standing nearby, is HOFFMAN, the fattish proprietor.

Strauss yawns, looks at his heavy, old-fashioned watch- and then, finishing his beer, rises from the table with a "good-night" which we do not hear and to which the others, lost in their game, make no response. Hoffman pantomimes "good-night."

As Strauss starts toward the exit, the CAMERA MOVES ALONG until the tavern door comes into view, ANGLING WITH Strauss as he comes through to show his progress down the street.

As his FOOTSTEPS break the otherwise silent night, the CAMERA CONTINUES ANGLING until the opposite side of the narrow street is brought into view. There, emerging from the shadows which have concealed him, appears Niemann.

                NIEMANN
    Herr Strauss...!

302   MED. CLOSE SHOT - STRAUSS

Strauss stops and turns to look back, puzzled by the voice and the unfamiliar figure coming toward him.

                STRAUSS
    What do you want?

Close to Strauss, Niemann strikes a match and holds it so that his face is fully illuminated.

                NIEMANN
    Do you remember me...?

                STRAUSS
    Doctor Niemann!

                NIEMANN
       (the cat, with a mouse)
    Yes, Heinrich -- Doctor Niemann.

As Strauss stares, Daniel COMES INTO VIEW behind him. His long arms reach out and his widespread fingers are near Strauss' neck as the CAMERA PANS AWAY to Niemann.

                        CONTINUED

302   CONTINUED

There is a cold, unemotional smile on his face as a choking gasp is HEARD, OFFSCENE. The CAMERA ANGLES with Niemann as he moves toward the Lampini living-wagon, dimly visible a little distance UPSCENE.

                                        WIPE INTO

303   INT. LAMPINI LIVING-WAGON- FULL SHOT

The only illumination is from a shaded lamp, turned low.

The ANGLE IS ACROSS THE BUNK toward the door through which Niemann is ENTERING, followed by Daniel. He carries Strauss' body over his shoulders. At a nod from Niemann, Daniel lets the limp body slide to the floor, where it lands in a grotesque heap.

As Daniel EXITS and closes the door, Niemann sits on the edge of the bunk - in which lies Ullman, his old assistant. Ullman is a little younger than Niemann, a rather intelligent type. His arms and legs are bound, and a handkerchief is tied across his mouth.

                    NIEMANN
              (nodding toward Strauss' body)
          Strauss -- the garrulous gentleman who
          saw me in the graveyard...He won't be
          much company for you, I'm afraid...

Ullman's fear-dilated eyes stare up at Niemann as he starts to untie the handkerchief.

304   EXT. VISARIA STREET - MED. FULL SHOT - NIGHT

The Lampini living-wagon rattles over the cobble stones and disappears around a corner...

305   INT. LAMPINI LIVING-WAGON - CLOSE SHOT - NIEMANN AND ULLMAN

Niemann, removing the handkerchief from about Ullman's mouth, becomes sarcastically solicitous as he raises the man to a sitting position and puts a pillow behind his back.

                    NIEMANN
          Is that more comfortable?

                    ULLMAN
              (finding voice)
          Niemann...! I've saved fifteen
          thousand marks since -

                                        CONTINUED

305   CONTINUED

> NIEMANN
> (finishing the line)
> Since you helped send me to prison?

> ULLMAN
> Let me go, and they're yours -- every one of them!

> NIEMANN
> (apparently considering this)
> A thousand marks a year -- for each of the fifteen I spent in a slimy, stinking dungeon...You bargain poorly, Herr Ullman.

> ULLMAN
> Don't kill me, Niemann! Don't!

> NIEMANN
> Kill you...? No, my friend -- I'm going to repay you for your treachery...
> (tapping Ullman's forehead)
> I'm going to give that brain of yours a new home --
> (smiling evilly)
> -- in the skull of the Frankenstein Monster...

> ULLMAN
> No, Niemann! No! No!

He breaks into an hysteria of half-crazed LAUGHTER as the SCENE

DISSOLVES INTO

306   INT. NIEMANN'S LABORATORY - FULL SHOT - NIGHT

The illumination is a cone of light from a large reflector lamp, above one of the operating tables beside which stand Niemann and Daniel. Both wear surgeons' coats.

The action is far UPSCENE, so that the operation in progress is presented only by suggestion. Niemann's back is also to CAMERA, completely concealing anything of a gruesome nature.

The surgery is apparently completed - for as the CAMERA STARTS TO TRUCK UPSCENE, Niemann leaves the table, carrying a large glass jar. As he moves toward a metal stand a little distance away, Daniel draws the sheet over the body, and rolls the wheeled table across the room.

307   MED. CLOSE SHOT - DANIEL

The CAMERA PANS with Daniel as he rolls the table to a point where a refrigerator-like door is set into the wall.

As he opens the door, a light automatically SNAPS on inside. The CAMERA ANGLES AROUND, to show the nature of the small room, beyond. Its walls are lined with frost-incrusted pipes. A body lies on another wheeled table, covered by a sheet.

Daniel rolls the operating table into the cold-room beside the first one - then steps back into the laboratory, closing the heavy door and fastening it.

308   MED. CLOSE SHOT - NIEMANN AT METAL STAND

His body still conceals the jar which he brought with him from the operating table.

On the stand is apparatus consisting of a small elevated glass tank, the contents of which pass through a glass tube connected to a small circulating pump, which is operated by a motor. From the pump extends another tube, through which the aerated output passes in small, rapidly traveling bubbles which are illuminated by a lamp, on the table.

Daniel, crossing from the cold-room, comes to where Niemann is at work.

Niemann steps aside, revealing two glass jars on the stand. In each, at rest in a clear watery solution, is a human brain. On one is a label upon which in printed letters is the name, STRAUSS. The other is labeled, ULLMAN.

It is now seen that the bubbling fluid from the pump continues to a "Y", supported by a laboratory clamp. From each leg of the "Y" are connections to "burettes", whose glass stoppers Niemann is regulating so that the liquid coming into them from the pump, falls drop by drop into the jars containing the brains.

A second pump returns the solution from the jars through other glass tubes to the tank above, from which it came.

Completing the adjustments, Niemann turns to Daniel.

       NIEMANN
   The plasma must flow at exactly this
   rate. If there is any change, call me.
   I will be in my study...

As he EXITS, the CAMERA MOVES UP CLOSER, so that the brains in the jars may be more clearly seen. Agitated slightly by the circulating plasma, they seem almost alive.

309   CLOSE SHOT - DANIEL

Awed by the results of Niemann's surgery, Daniel bends closer to inspect the brains. He reacts with a sudden start to the SOUND of:

> ILONKA'S VOICE
> Daniel...?

As he turns, the CAMERA WHIPS TOWARD the corridor platform, where Ilonka is coming down the stairs into the laboratory.

310   MED. CLOSE SHOT - ILONKA

The CAMERA PANS with Ilonka as she moves toward Daniel.

> ILONKA (continued)
> Have you seen Larry...?

As Daniel ENTERS from the opposite direction, the CAMERA STOPS, holding him and Ilonka in a MEDIUM CLOSE SHOT.

Daniel doesn't answer Ilonka. He fixes his eyes on her, consumed by jealousy.

> ILONKA
> What's the matter with you, Daniel?

Daniel's pent up jealousy suddenly pours forth. He closes his fingers in a hard grip around Ilonka's wrist.

> DANIEL
> You like Larry, don't you!? You don't like me, because I'm an ugly hunchback...!

> ILONKA
> (angrily)
> You're hurting me!
> (she tries to free herself)

> DANIEL
> You love him! Don't lie to me! I've seen it! You love him!

> ILONKA
> Yes, I do!
> (jerking her hand free)

> DANIEL
> He's a werewolf! When the change comes, he'll kill you!

> ILONKA
> (enraged)
> I hate you!

CONTINUED

310 CONTINUED

As she turns abruptly and runs toward the stairs, the CAMERA MOVES CLOSER TO DANIEL. He looks after her for a moment and then, in a PAN SHOT, moves toward the table on which the Monster lies, concealed by the steam in the case which covers him.

Turning the valve on the autoclave, Daniel shuts off the steam - then operates the block and tackle. As the case raises above the table, the released vapor escapes, exposing the Monster. Daniel steps closer to the table, looking down at --

311 CLOSE DOWNWARD ANGLE ON MONSTER'S FACE

Since last seen, a subtle change has taken place in the grotesque face. It appears to be more alive...

312 CLOSE SHOT - DANIEL

His face distorts with rage.

313 MED. CLOSE FOREGROUND SHOT - MONSTER'S TABLE

With a vicious snarl, Daniel grabs one of the long leather straps which bind the monster to the table and, with mad strength, tears it from its metal ring.

>   DANIEL
> If it weren't for you, I'd have
> the Wolf Man's body!

He starts flailing the Monster with bestial fury....

314 CLOSE SHOT - MONSTER

As Daniel's punishment continues, the Monster's eyelids slowly open. Baleful wrath comes into his eyes as they turn in a sidelong glance toward Daniel...

315 MED. CLOSE FOREGROUND SHOT - MONSTER'S TABLE

Daniel's merciless castigation of the creature he hates continues as the SCENE

FADES OUT

316   INT. TAVERN - MED. CLOSE - NEAR COUNTER - DAY

As the scene FADES IN, Hoffman is behind the barcounter at the old-fashioned wall telephone. Several villagers of different types are having their noonday beers.

> HOFFMAN
> Yes, Mrs. Strauss...
> (pause)
> No, Mrs. Strauss...
> (bored)
> He was here last night, but I haven't seen him this morning...
> (pause)
> If I do, I'll tell him...

During this, the CAMERA ANGLES AWAY to a little table near the window at which sit TOBERMAN, the Burgemaster, and INSPECTOR MULLER, of the local Police Department. Toberman is a well set up man of fifty. Muller is younger. They are eating lunch.

> HOFFMAN'S VOICE (continued)
> Yes, Mrs. Strauss....
> (pause)
> Yes, yes, yes, Mrs. Strauss...

> TOBERMAN
> (impatiently)
> Our beers, Hoffman!

317   CLOSE SHOT - HOFFMAN

> HOFFMAN
> (looking off)
> Right away, Herr Burgomaster!
> (into phone)
> I've got to go, Mrs. Strauss!..
> Goodbye!

He hangs up and turns to the counter, picking up a tray on which are two steins of beer.

> HOFFMAN
> I don't know why --

18   MED. SHOT - TOBERMAN AND MULLER

They are looking toward Hoffman as he approaches the table.

CONTINUED

318 CONTINUED

> HOFFMAN (continued)
> -- the housewives of Visaria should ask me where their husbands are, all the time...!

> TOBERMAN
> (amused)
> What now, Hoffman?

> HOFFMAN
> (as he serves them)
> Strauss hasn't been home since yesterday. His wife's worried...

> TOBERMAN
> Sleeping off a drunk, probably.

> MULLER
> (in a low voice, as Hoffman exits)
> I don't think so...

> TOBERMAN
> Why not?
> (drinks beer)

> MULLER
> Ullman hasn't been home since last night -- and neither has Braun, the storekeeper...

> TOBERMAN
> (frowning)
> Humph! Odd.

> MULLER
> When one man doesn't come home, you think nothing of it. When three disappear overnight -- particularly in a small place like Visaria -- you begin to wonder...

> HERTZ' VOICE
> Inspector! Inspector!

Toberman and Muller look up as HERTZ ENTERS. He is a gnarled old woodcutter, whose obvious agitation spreads through the little tavern in a flash.

> HERTZ (continued)
> I've found Herr Braun, Inspector!
> (gasping for breath)
> Out in the woods...!

CONTINUED

318 CONTINUED - 2

Toberman and Muller spring to their feet. The villagers become infected by the old man's excitement, as the scene

DISSOLVES INTO

319 EXT. WOODS - MED. FOREGROUND SHOT - DAY

Toberman, Muller and DOCTOR GEISSLER are huddled over Braun's body, the upper half of which lies in a natural depression, concealed from view. Geissler, the Village doctor, is a man of sixty or so.

Old Hertz and the villagers seen in the tavern are standing in hushed little groups, awed in the presence of death.

> TOBERMAN
> What do you make of it, Doctor....?
>
> GEISSLER
> The jugular vein is severed...
> (looking up)
> Not cut, but torn apart -- as though by powerful teeth...
>
> HERTZ
> (excitedly)
> A wolf! I heard one in these woods, last night!
>
> MULLER
> There haven't been wolves in Visaria since I can remember!
>
> HERTZ
> I heard the howl of a wolf, I tell you! There was something unearthly about it, too! It sounded --
> (in a quaking voice)
> -- almost human...
>
> SCHWARTZ
> (A werewolf!
> (
> (AD LIBS
> (A werewolf!
> (We'll all be murdered!
> (Heaven help us!
> (
> (MEIER
> (I must warn my wife and children!
> (
> (SCHWARTZ
> (Me, too!

CONTINUED

319   CONTINUED

Schwartz and Meier start to leave. Toberman calls, angrily.

                    TOBERMAN
      Schwartz! Meier! Come back here!

The authoritative note in Toberman's voice silences the villagers and brings Meier and Schwartz back to the group.

320   CLOSE SHOT - TOBERMAN AND MULIER

                    TOBERMAN
      I forbid that you spread any such talk!
      What do you want to do!? Drive people
      away from Visaria and ruin our village
      forever!?

321   GROUP SHOT

                    TOBERMAN (continued)
      I'm surprised at you!
          (sweeping the group with
           his eyes)
      All of you! Believing in such an
      idiotic superstition!

                    SCHWARTZ
          (pointing to Braun's body)
      How do you explain <u>that</u>!?

                    MEIER
      And what about Strauss?

                    SCHWARTZ
      And Ullman? What happened to <u>them</u>!?
      If there's a werewolf, our people
      should know about it.

The other villagers nod and murmur unintelligible AD LIBS.

                    VILLAGERS
      (Our children aren't safe...
      (I think so too, Herr Burgomaster...
AD LIB (I'm with you, Schwartz!
      (If there's a werewolf, let's find him!
      (Aye! Search for the werewolf!

                            CONTINUED

321   CONTINUED

>   TOBERMAN
>   All right! All right!
>   (to Muller, as the villagers
>   quiet down)
>   Organize searching parties, Inspector...
>   We'll head one group --
>   (toward the others)
>   Schwartz, another -- and Meier, a third.
>   (loudly, above murmurs
>   of approval)
>   <u>Find</u> your werewolf!

On this, the scene is

>   DISSOLVING INTO

322   INT. NIEMANN'S GARDEN - CLOSEUP ON GROUND - <u>DAY</u>

The DISSOLVE COMES IN ON A CLOSE DOWNWARD ANGLE showing a piece of branchwood held by an unseen hand as it traces the sign of the pentagram in the earth. At the same time, the CAMERA IS PULLING BACK AND ANGLING UPWARD, revealing Larry. He is seated on a stone bench beside the path.

In the depths of profound anguish, Larry flings the branchwood away and holds his head between his hands, closing his eyes tightly as though to shut out his tormenting thoughts.

SOUNDS of FOOTSTEPS are heard, coming near. Ilonka ENTERS She looks at Larry with deep compassion - then sits quietly beside him.

>   ILONKA
>   Larry....?
>
>   LARRY
>   (staring at the ground)
>   Last night -- I killed a man...

Ilonka tries to choke a gasp of horror - a reaction which gives way to contrite sympathy as Larry faces her in bleak despair.

>   LARRY (continued)
>   (almost a sob)
>   I want to die...
>
>   ILONKA
>   You mustn't say that! You didn't
>   know what you were doing!

>   CONTINUED

322   CONTINUED

>   LARRY
>   But I did! I wanted to kill!
>   And I <u>knew</u> that I wanted to!
>   (looking skyward)
>   The moon will rise again tonight...
>   (facing her)
>   When it does, I'll become the beast
>   again -- and I'll kill, kill, <u>kill</u>!
>
>   ILONKA
>   I won't let you! I won't let you
>   out of my sight!
>
>   LARRY
>   (frenziedly)
>   I'd kill you! I couldn't help myself...!
>
>   ILONKA
>   But Doctor Niemann will cure you!
>   You said that he would!
>
>   LARRY
>   I want to die...!
>   (springs to his feet)

323   CLOSE SHOT - LARRY

>   LARRY (continued)
>   It's the only way my soul can find
>   peace! Don't you understand? I <u>can't</u>
>   go on waiting - and killing -- and
>   waiting! I want forgetfulness and <u>peace</u>!

324   CLOSE SHOT - ILONKA

Moved beyond words, Ilonka bites her lip and tries to
blink back the tears which glisten in her eyes as:

>   LARRY'S VOICE (continues)
>   But a werewolf can't just <u>die</u> --

325   LARGER SHOT - LARRY AND ILONKA

>   LARRY (continues)
>   -- he must be <u>killed</u>. He must die
>   by a silver bullet --
>   (he drops to the ground
>   upon his knees and buries
>   his face upon his arm, in
>   Ilonka's lap)
>   -- fired by someone who loves him
>   enough to understand - and who would
>   want him to find release...

CONTINUED

cs

325 CONTINUED

During this, the CAMERA HAS MOVED closer to Ilonka. As she rests a hand upon Larry's head, her other hand comes up to the necklace of coins about her throat. The CAMERA IS MOVING STILL CLOSER as her fingers close upon one of the coins, brighter than the others.

Ilonka is looking into space through her tears as the scene

DISSOLVES INTO

326 EXT. CLOSEUP - ROCK ON GROUND - DAY

As the scene DISSOLVES IN, Ilonka's hand comes into view holding the bright metal coin from her necklace on its edge upon the rock. Using a rusty old hammer, she pounds the coin into the approximate form of a silver bullet as the scene

DISSOLVES INTO

327 INT. NIEMANN'S GUN ROOM - RACK - CLOSE SHOT - DAY

This shows a collection of Medieval firearms, supported by pegs set into the wooden panel of the wall.

As Ilonka ENTERS, the CAMERA MOVES toward the panel and loses her from view, continuing its movement until a small, single-barrel pistol, of the Derringer type, is brought into view. As Ilonka's hand comes into the picture and takes the pistol from its pegs,

DISSOLVE INTO

328 INT. NIEMANN'S LABORATORY - MED. SHOT - NIGHT

The Monster lies on the operating table, covered by the glass case. Since last seen, certain alterations have been made in the case.

In its sides, near the head and feet of the Monster, long porcelain insulator-conductors pass through the glass, with similar conductors in each of the ends. Inside the case, each of the conductor rods terminate in a 3" disc of metal.

Outside, one of the long high-frequency cables suspended from a supporting rack, is attached in "series" to the metal rods which pass through the insulators.

CONTINUED

328   CONTINUED

The second high-frequency lead passes into the case through a 7th insulator-conductor at the Monster's feet and, inside, is connected to a metal plate on which the Monster lies, strapped. Both high-frequency leads continue from the distributor panel to the Tesla high-frequency apparatus, nearby.

As the scene DISSOLVES IN, Niemann is connecting "parallel" leads from the Tesla generator to the rotating spark gap. Daniel, near at hand, is looking at the Monster with smoldering rage. During the business, the door opposite the stair landing opens and Larry ENTERS.

329   CLOSE SHOT - LARRY

In his drawn expression is reflected the emotional turmoil he has suffered during the past twenty-four hours.

The CAMERA PANS with him as he moves across the room to the Monster's table, where Niemann has now completed the various connections and, with all the intensity of the true scientist, stands ready to try his final experiment.

> NIEMANN
> (to Daniel)
> Start the generator.....

Daniel goes to where the stem of a valve comes up through the floor to a large, iron control wheel. During this, Larry steps closer to the table and looks at the complicated arrangement of wires.

330   CLOSE SHOT - DANIEL

He is turning the control wheel of the valve.

331   INT. BASEMENT ROOM - TURBINE GENERATOR (MIN.) - CLOSE SHOT

Set into the 18" feedline which comes through the wall is a large "gate" valve, the stem from which extends upward through a hole in the ceiling.

From the valve a feedline elbows downward to a water-turbine, connected by a shaft to a high-frequency generator

As the stem of the valve turns, a rush of water is heard and the generator armature starts turning.

cs

332   EXT. MASONRY WALL - SLUICE OPENING - (MIN.) - MED. CLOSE SHOT

Water begins to pour through the spillway.

333   INT. NIEMANN'S LABORATORY - DANIEL - CLOSE SHOT

He continues turning the valve wheel.

334   EXT. MASONRY WALL - SLUICE OPENING - CLOSE SHOT

As the pressure increases, the water shoots from the opening in a solid jet.

335   INT. BASEMENT ROOM - TURBINE GENERATOR - CLOSER SHOT

The speed of the armature increases until its sound becomes a whine.

336   INT. NIEMANN'S LABORATORY - NEAR OPERATING TABLE - MED. CLOSE

Larry watches Niemann, while he makes certain that all the high-frequency terminals are tight.

>   LARRY
> If the atomic charge isn't strong enough...
>
>   NIEMANN
>   (interrupting, angrily)
> It will succeed! The electronic bombardment will penetrate every tissue in his body and charge it with a force greater than he ever possessed!

He steps to the switchboard and looks at --

337   CLOSEUP - MEGA-VOLTMETER

The needle is climbing toward the 25,000 point.

338   MED. SHOT - MONSTER'S TABLE

As Niemann closes the master switch, the high-frequency currents discharge across the rods of the spreading gap. Following this, Niemann closes the switch which starts the motor of the rotating gap - and then, when the motor has reached full speed, cuts in the switch which feeds the high-frequency circuit into it. As the discharges across the gap blend into a circle of light, Niemann puts his hand out to a fourth switch, and turns toward the Monster's case....

339 CLOSEUP - SWITCH

Niemann's hand closes the switch.

340 CLOSE SHOT - MONSTER'S CASE

As the current begins to flow, high-frequency "trees" begin to crackle from the disc electrodes. They continue to grow with the increase in voltage, until at last the Monster is enveloped from head to feet in a network of flaming sparks which form strange and ever-changing patterns.

341 MED. SHOT

Larry watches with Niemann, who is observing the effect with fanatical eyes. He calls to Daniel.

                    NIEMANN
  More power....

342 CLOSE SHOT - DANIEL

He gives the wheel of the valve another turn.

343 INT. BASEMENT ROOM - TURBINE GENERATOR - CLOSE SHOT

As the speed increases, sparks from the brushes form a continuous circle of light around the commutator.

344 INT. NIEMANN'S LABORATORY - MEGA-VOLTMETER - CLOSEUP

The needle is moving toward the 50,000 mark.

345 MED. SHOT - MONSTER'S TABLE

As the voltage increases, the network of sparks playing over the Monster becomes a more closely knit pattern, until finally his body is enveloped in an aura which becomes brighter and brighter until it appears that the body is being consumed.

                    LARRY
              (after a few seconds)
  How long -- will it take...?

CONTINUED

345 CONTINUED

> NIEMANN
> (intent on
> watching)
> What?
> (as Larry's question
> registers)
> I don't know...
>
> LARRY
> The moon will be full, at midnight...
> (tormented)
> Can you operate, before then?
>
> NIEMANN
> I don't know, I tell you!
> (then, in a
> gentler manner)
> You will need all your strength,
> my boy. Go to your room and rest....
>
> LARRY
> You must do it before midnight!
> You must!
>
> NIEMANN
> Do as I tell you! When the time
> comes, I will call you.

As Larry flings himself away from the table and EXITS, Daniel leaves the valve and comes to foreground, where he watches the proceedings with impressed awe.

Niemann steps to the switchboard...

346 CLOSE SHOT - MEGA-VOLTMETER

Niemann's hand comes into the picture and turns the regulating wheel toward "Increase". The needle on the meter climbs beyond the 75,000 mark...

347 MED. SHOT - MONSTER'S TABLE

As the high-frequency effects increase in intensity, Niemann bends over the Monster's case to observe the effect.

348 INT. BASEMENT ROOM - TURBINE GENERATOR - CLOSE SHOT

The whine of the generator is becoming a piercing shriek.

b1

349   INT. NIEMANN'S LABORATORY - MED. CLOSE - OPERATING
        TABLE

        A buzzer suddenly begins to sound, off scene. Niemann
        looks toward the switchboard.

350   MEGA-VOLTMETER - CLOSEUP

        The needle has passed the 100,000 mark and the word "DANGER"
        is flashing on and off, illuminated by the light behind it.

351   INT. BASEMENT ROOM - TURBINE GENERATOR - CLOSE SHOT

        The coils of the generator begin to smoke. A large, open
        type circuit-breaker on the wall kicks out and a curling,
        blinding flame of light arcs across the carbon terminals...

352   EXT. NIEMANN'S GARDEN - FULL SHOT

        Pencils of light shaft through the bars of a small basement
        window close to the ground, flooding the garden with weird,
        continually shifting spots of brilliance and darkness....

353   EXT. OUTSIDE WALL OF NIEMANN'S GARDEN - FULL SHOT

        The high wall is on the left. It terminates at a corner,
        some distance upscene. Beyond the corner is a disused
        road, on the other side of which grows tall, dry marsh
        grass in rank profusion.

        The shifting beams of light, breaking over the garden wall
        in upward angles, illuminate the scene with a ghostly
        effect, revealing Meier and another villager, BORN,
        standing in the foreground, staring, rooted to the spot by
        fear....

354   INT. NIEMANN'S LABORATORY - NEAR MONSTER'S TABLE - MED.
        CLOSE SHOT

        All the high-frequency effects have ceased. Niemann,
        turning the voltage regulating wheel in the "DECREASE"
        direction, hurriedly opens the master switch....

355   INT. BASEMENT ROOM - TURBINE GENERATOR - CLOSE SHOT

        The arc goes out and the arm of the circuit-breaker snaps
        back into contact, completing the circuit....

bl

356 INT. NIEMANN'S LABORATORY - NEAR MONSTER'S TABLE - MED. CLOSE SHOT

All of the high-frequency effects resume. Niemann, watching the Monster's case, turns the voltage regulator wheel slowly in the "INCREASE" direction...

357 EXT. OUTSIDE WALL OF NIEMANN'S GARDEN - BORN - CLOSE SHOT

Not understanding what they have seen, but in the belief that they have witnessed some supernatural phenomenon, Meier and Born run toward the road and disappear among the trees on the right.

358 INT. NIEMANN'S LABORATORY - MONSTER'S TABLE - MED. CLOSE

Niemann, alternately watching the Monster's case and the voltmeter, slowly increases the current.

As the CAMERA MOVES TOWARD THE TABLE, the aura of light which bathes the Monster is coming up to full intensity again as the scene

DISSOLVES INTO

359 EXT. WOODS - MED. FULL SHOT - NIGHT

A number of villagers, headed by Schwartz, are coming through the woods from various directions, converging toward the point where Burgomaster Toberman and Inspector Muller are entering in MEDIUM FOREGROUND. Some of the villagers carry lighted torches. All are armed.

     TOBERMAN
    (as Schwartz joins
     them)
Any sign of your werewolf...?

     SCHWARTZ
    (uneasily)
We're early for him, I guess...

     TOBERMAN
    (scoffingly)
Hah! So he appears on schedule - like a train? Is that it?

     MEIER'S VOICE
Herr Toberman! Inspector Muller!

All look off, reacting as they start out --

b1

360   MED. SHOT - WOODS

Meier and Born are running in a PAN SHOT which
progresses them toward the group...

361   TOBERMAN, MULLER, ET AL. - MED. SHOT

They are running in a PAN SHOT which now includes Meier and
Born, coming nearer...

362   GROUP SHOT

Meier, and Born, breathless, enter from left as Toberman,
Muller and the others enter from right.

> MEIER
> (gasping, excitedly)
> Lights! At Doctor Niemann's!
>
> BORN
> (equally excited)
> Weird lights!
>
> MEIER
> Flashing all over the place!
>
> TOBERMAN
> At Doctor Niemann's!?
>
> MEIER
> In the garden!
>
> BORN
> We saw them from the road...!
>
> MULLER
> His place has been closed for fifteen
> years...!
>
> TOBERMAN
> Ever since Niemann went to prison...
>
> MEIER
> Something's going on up there, I
> tell you!
>
> TOBERMAN
> We'll see...

The group is already on its way in a PAN SHOT as the scene

DISSOLVES INTO

INT. LARRY'S ROOM - CLOSEUP - FLOOR - NIGHT

The CAMERA IS ANGLING DOWNWARD on a CLOSE SHOT of Larry's feet. His shoes and socks have been removed, and the change from human feet to those of a werewolf is already in progress - a metamorphosis during which his toes become those of an animal's foot, covered by a hairy growth... During this change, the CAMERA PULLS BACK into a LARGER SHOT. There is only a single light in the room - a shaded lamp, on the dresser.

Larry, seated on the edge of the bed, has his head bent over as he stares at his feet.

A sob of agony chokes in his throat as he moves in a PAN SHOT to the dresser, to look at his reflection in the mirror. He feels his face...

          LARRY
       (almost inaudibly)
  No, no!....No!

64   INT. HALL IN NIEMANN'S CASTLE - MED. CLOSE - LARRY'S DOOR

Ilonka enters. She hesitates - then knocks on the door.

          ILONKA
  Larry...

65   INT. LARRY'S ROOM - MED. CLOSE - LARRY AT DRESSER

A hairy growth is now beginning to show on Larry's face. As he hears Ilonka's voice, he turns toward the door.

          LARRY
  Go away!

          ILONKA'S VOICE
  No, Larry! Let me in!

As Larry turns to the dresser without answering, the CAMERA MOVES toward the mirror and, in a DISSOLVE IN ACTION continues Larry's change into the Wolf Man -- a gradual transmutation which brings snarling and labored breathing.

          ILONKA'S VOICE
  Larry! Larry!

Larry turns toward the door. When he speaks, there is only a trace of anything human in his snarling voice.

          LARRY
  Go away!

b1

366   INT. HALL IN NIEMANN'S CASTLE - CLOSE SHOT - ILONKA
      AT DOOR

   Realizing that the change is taking place, Ilonka runs
   out of the scene with a choked cry.

367   INT. NIEMANN'S LABORATORY - MONSTER'S TABLE - MED. SHOT

   Niemann and Daniel stand near the case in which the
   Monster's body still lies, enveloped in a brilliant aura
   of light.

   Niemann bends closer, shading his eyes against the light
   as he looks down at --

368   CLOSE DOWNWARD ANGLE ON MONSTER

   The Monster's face appears strangely alive. Now, his
   eyes open wide and glow with a baleful light as he stares
   up into the face of the man who has brought him back to
   life.

369   MED. SHOT - MONSTER'S TABLE

   Niemann, seeing that his experiment has succeeded, turns
   to the switchboard and opens the master switch. As he
   does so, the high-tenson effects cease and the aura of
   light around the Monster instantly disappears.

                  NIEMANN
               (to Daniel)
         Raise the case....

   Daniel starts to operate the block and tackle...

370   EXT. NIEMANN'S GARDEN - MED. CLOSE - CASTLE ENTRANCE

   The large, nail-studded doors, swing open. Light floods
   the terrace as Ilonka runs out, into the garden...

371   CLOSE SHOT - ILONKA

   Moved by her deep concern for Larry, she bites her lip
   as she looks off toward --

372   FRENCH DOORS TO LARRY'S ROOM - MED. SHOT

   -- as from Ilonka's angle. The doors are closed....

bl

373 CLOSE SHOT - ILONKA

She hesitates -- then runs toward the doors of Larry's room --

374 FRENCH DOORS TO LARRY'S ROOM - MED. CLOSE SHOT

Ilonka enters and knocks frantically on the doors.

ILONKA
Larry...! Larry!

375 INT. LARRY'S ROOM - CLOSE SHOT - LARRY AT DRESSER

As he looks at his reflection in the mirror and another DISSOLVE continues his change into the werewolf, Larry's labored breathing becomes a guttural snarl...

376 INT. NIEMANN'S LABORATORY - MONSTER'S TABLE - MED. CLOSE

The case is now high above the table beside which stands Niemann, looking down into the Monster's eyes...

377 CLOSEUP - MONSTER

The Monster glares up at Niemann, then shifts his eyes toward --

378 CLOSE SHOT - DANIEL

A FLASH of Daniel, seen from the Monster's angle...

379 CLOSE SHOT - MONSTER

As he remembers the man who tortured him, a snarl of rage comes from the Monster's throat.

380 MED. CLOSE

Daniel recoils in fear as the Gargantuan figure strains against the straps which bind him to the metal plate.

Niemann, seeing that the Monster's energies have been restored, experiences all the elation of the true scientist

NIEMANN
Tell the Wolf Man I am ready...

CONTINUED

CONTINUED

                   DANIEL
     Master...
          (as Niemann looks up)
     Let the Monster have _my_ brain...

The Monster turns his head, following Daniel's movement as he comes around the table, closer to Niemann.

                DANIEL (cont'd)
     ...give _me_ the Wolf Man's body...

                NIEMANN
          (infuriated)
     Do as I tell you!

                DANIEL
          (after a surly pause)
     Yes, Master...

As he starts toward the door, Niemann looks after him for a moment -- then turns to the Monster, who continues snarling as he strains to break the straps.....

INT. LARRY'S ROOM - MED. CLOSE SHOT - LARRY AT DRESSER

The _change_ is now complete. Snarling at his wolfish image, Larry leaves the dresser and in a PAN SHOT reaches the garden doors and flings them open...

EXT. NIEMANN'S GARDEN - FRENCH DOORS TO LARRY'S ROOM - MED. SHOT

As the doors fly open and bang against the wall, Larry steps out onto the terrace, snarling and baring his teeth as he sees Ilonka.

CLOSE SHOT - ILONKA

She drops back with an inarticulate gasp as she sees the revolting transformation that has taken place in Larry....

CLOSE SHOT - LARRY

His labored breathing becomes faster and faster. Unable to resist any longer the werewolf's impulse to kill, he starts slowly toward Ilonka, moving in a PAN SHOT which brings her into view.

Contrite horror comes into Ilonka's face as the inhuman beast that once was Larry, pauses, snarling, only a few feet from her.....

385 INT. HALL IN NIEMANN'S CASTLE - MED. SHOT

Daniel is standing before the locked door of Larry's room, rattling the knob...

386 EXT. NIEMANN'S GARDEN - MED. CLOSE - LARRY AND ILONKA

There is no vestige of anything human in Larry as he takes a slow step toward Ilonka...

387 CLOSE SHOT - ILONKA

Understanding with full force Larry's desire for release, Ilonka draws the pistol from her pocket...

388 CLOSE SHOT - LARRY

As he sees Ilonka's movement with the pistol, Larry bares his fang-like teeth....

389 CLOSE SHOT - ILONKA

A sudden sob chokes in Ilonka's throat. Lacking courage to pull the trigger, she covers her face with her arm and, in a PAN SHOT, moves dazedly toward a tree, near the terrace

Larry comes into view, behind her. He hesitates for an instant - then, with a guttural snarl, he grabs Ilonka and drags her out of sight behind the tree.

The CAMERA HOLDS ON THIS FOR A FEW SECONDS, during which are heard sounds of snarling, and pitiful little sobs from Ilonka. Then comes the sound of a pistol shot --

390 WOODS - TOBERMAN, MULLER, ET AL.

As they react to the shot, the CAMERA IS PANNING with Toberman and the others as they pour down a wooded slope onto the disused road...

391 INT. HALL OF NIEMANN'S CASTLE - FULL SHOT

Daniel has also heard the shot and is running toward the turn of the upscene corridor...

392 EXT. NIEMANN'S GARDEN - MED. CLOSE SHOT - NEAR TREE

Ilonka is lying on the ground in a position to completely conceal the wounds inflicted upon her by the Wolf Man.

CONTINUED

92 CONTINUED

From offscene, are heard sounds of Larry dying -- and, as the CAMERA PANS AWAY from Ilonka, he is brought into view.

93 CLOSE DOWNWARD SHOT ON LARRY

His heavy, animal-like breathing ceases. His eyes close. As they do so, a DISSOLVE removes the hairy growth from his face and changes him again to Larry Talbot, the sufferer whose tortured soul has found at last the peace he sought.

94 CASTLE ENTRANCE - MED. SHOT

Daniel runs into the garden onto the terrace. A choked little cry comes to him from the direction of the tree, upscene...

95 MED. CLOSE - DOWNWARD ANGLE - ILONKA

     ILONKA
    (almost inaudibly)
 Larry...

With her last strength, she is pulling herself over the ground toward Larry.

Beside him now, Ilonka snuggles close and presses her cheek against his. As a little smile comes upon her face, the CAMERA ANGLES UP, to show Daniel, running toward foreground.

96 CLOSE SHOT - DANIEL

He stops, stunned as he looks down at --

97 CLOSE SHOT - LARRY AND ILONKA

As Ilonka's body relaxes in death, the smile fades from her face...

98 MED. CLOSE

Stricken by the only grief his warped mind has ever known, Daniel stoops down and lifts Ilonka's body tenderly in his arms. He looks into her face for a moment, then moves slowly across the garden in a PAN SHOT which brings the castle entrance into view....

399 ROAD - A LITTLE DISTANCE FROM NIEMANN'S CASTLE - MED. SHOT

Toberman and the other villagers are running along the overgrown road...

400 INT. NIEMANN'S LABORATORY - MED. SHOT - MONSTER'S TABLE

The Monster is snarling and straining at his bonds. Upscene, Niemann is near one of the other tables, preparing for the operation.

The CAMERA ANGLES AWAY from the Monster toward the door on the right, through which Daniel is now appearing, carrying Ilonka's body in his arms...

401 CLOSE SHOT - NIEMANN

Hearing Daniel's entrance, he turns to look toward the door, reacting as he sees...

402 MED. CLOSE - DANIEL

His gaze is fixed offscene toward Niemann, as he moves in a PAN SHOT which brings Niemann into view.

> NIEMANN
> What's happened?

> DANIEL
> (pausing)
> The Wolf Man killed her...

He places Ilonka's body tenderly upon the table - then turns to face Niemann, moving slowly toward him.

> DANIEL
> (quietly)
> If you had done as I asked you to, it wouldn't have happened...

At the instant Niemann realizes that the psychopathic killer is turning against him, Daniel's hands close about his throat.

> DANIEL
> Remember Professor Lampini...and Strauss...and Ullman...
> (as his hands close tighter)
> You're going to join them, Master...

CONTINUED)

as

402 CONTINUED

As Daniel's fingers tighten, Niemann's hands come up and close upon his wrists.

But Niemann's strength is no match for the hunchback's. Daniel's grip becomes tighter and tighter.

403 MED. CLOSE - MONSTER'S TABLE

The guttural growls which have been coming from the Monster during the preceding scene, climax in a snarl of fury.

With a sudden burst of strength which breaks the straps from his wrists, the Monster sits up, rips the bonds from his legs and swings off the table, body swaying as he turns upscene to face Niemann and Daniel.

404 CLOSE SHOT - MONSTER

All the fury of the criminal brain imprisoned in the Monster's skull comes into his eyes. In giant strides, he moves away from the table in a PAN SHOT which brings Niemann and Daniel into view.

405 MED. CLOSE - DANIEL AND NIEMANN

Niemann is trying to tear the hunchback's fingers from his throat as the Monster strides toward them. Both are unaware of his presence until the Monster, now close to Daniel, takes one final stride and, with both hands, grabs one of Daniel's arms and with a mighty jerk, tears his fingers from Niemann's throat.

As the Monster flings him aside, Daniel wheels to confront him.

406 CLOSE SHOT - MONSTER

A snarl of hatred comes from the Monster's throat.

406 CLOSE SHOT - DANIEL

Abject terror comes into the hunchback's expression.

                           DANIEL
                Master! Save me! Save me!

408 LARGER SHOT

As Daniel starts in a run across the room, Niemann, recovering his breath, tries to interpose himself between the Monster and Daniel. But the Monster, with a backhand swing of his arm, sweeps Niemann aside and, with a mighty shove, sends one of the apparatus tables skidding across the room after Daniel.

409 MED. PAN SHOT - APPARATUS STAND

The CAMERA ANGLES with the moving stand, showing that it overturns upon the hunchback as he loses his balance and falls to the floor.

410 CLOSE SHOT - DANIEL

He furiously tries to extricate himself from the apparatus while he looks off toward --

411 MED. CLOSE SHOT - MONSTER

As the giant figure strides toward CAMERA, Niemann tries to stop him again. Without pausing, the Monster hurls him away.

412 CLOSE SHOT - FLOOR

As Niemann falls into the picture, his head hits the corner of the operating table and he is knocked unconscious.

413 CLOSE SHOT - MONSTER

He strides inexorably onward in a PAN SHOT which brings Daniel into view. Just as Daniel extricates himself from the apparatus, the Monster seizes him and jerks him to his feet.

414 EXT. NIEMANN'S GARDEN - MED. FULL SHOT

The villagers' torches light the garden weirdly as they follow Toberman and Muller in a PAN SHOT which progresses them toward the castle entrance...

415 INT. NIEMANN'S LABORATORY - MED. FULL SHOT

The Monster has the frantically screaming hunchback in his arms and is striding toward the large window, upscene.

416   CLOSE SHOT - MONSTER AND DANIEL

      Daniel screams wildly as the Monster raises him into
      the air.

417   MED. SHOT TOWARD WINDOW

      The Monster hurls Daniel's body toward the window.

418   EXT. NIEMANN'S GARDEN - MED. SHOT NEAR CASTLE ENTRANCE

      Toberman and the villagers come to a startled halt as
      Daniel's body crashes through the window and hurtles
      downward upon the flagstones.

419   INT. NIEMANN'S LABORATORY - CLOSE SHOT - NIEMANN

      Niemann drags himself dazedly to his feet, reacting as
      hears the snarl of the Monster, now coming toward him
      from the window.

      He staggers blindly toward the stair platform in a
      PAN SHOT which brings the Monster into view, intercepting
      him.

420   CLOSEUP - MONSTER

      He looks off toward Niemann - then starts toward him,
      snarling.

421   MED. CLOSE SHOT - NIEMANN

      Niemann turns in fear and starts across the room. The
      Monster, moving with fast strides, catches up with him
      and seizes him with a triumphant bellow of rage.

422   EXT. NIEMANN'S GARDEN - MED. SHOT - ENTRANCE TO CASTLE

      As Toberman and the villagers hear <u>Niemann's offscene
      scream</u>, they pour through the castle entrance.

423   INT. NIEMANN'S LABORATORY - MED. SHOT - MONSTER

      Holding Niemann under one arm, the Monster is moving in
      giant strides toward the stair platform.

as

424   MED. CLOSE SHOT - STAIR PLATFORM

Toberman and the villagers appear from the hall, stopping in frozen amazement as they see --

425   CLOSE SHOT - MONSTER AND NIEMANN

Niemann, struggling to free himself from the Monster's vise-like hold, reacts to those who have entered:

> NIEMANN
> (screaming wildly)
> It's the Frankenstein Monster! Help me! Help me!

Still dazed from his fall, Niemann loses consciousness.

As the Monster sees the men, he snarls and backs away.

426   MED. SHOT - TOBERMAN AND VILLAGERS

Several of the men in the rear flee in terror. One hurls his flaming torch.

427   MED. CLOSE - MONSTER

As the torch hurtles into the scene and blazes on the floor in front of the Monster, he gives a snarl of fear. Grabbing one of the nearby metal stands, he hurls it with all his mighty strength.

428   MED. SHOT - TOBERMAN AND VILLAGERS

As the stand comes flying into the scene, the villagers surge back into the corridor - but not before several of them have been hit.

429   FULL SHOT

The Monster is stomping across the room with Niemann, exiting through the door on the right as the villagers pour down the stairs and start after him.

430   INT. HALL IN NIEMANN'S CASTLE - FULL SHOT

Holding Niemann's form under his arm like a sack of meal, the Monster crosses the hall in giant strides, kicks open the door of Larry's room and exits into it as the villagers come in from the laboratory.

as

431   EXT. NIEMANN'S GARDEN - FULL SHOT

       The Monster comes from Larry's room and strides toward the gate. As he nears it, some of the villagers, now rushing into the garden from Larry's room, pick up stones and hurl them. Others throw their torches.

432   MED. CLOSE - MONSTER NEAR GATE

       Some of the stones hit the Monster. He turns away in rage, snarling and fleeing in terror through the gate as the torches land flaming at his feet.

433   MED. FULL SHOT

       The villagers continue across the garden toward the gate.

434   EXT. OUTSIDE WALL OF NIEMANN'S GARDEN - MED. SHOT - <u>NIGHT</u>

       The Monster, carrying Niemann, is striding thunderously upscene as the villagers come through the gate, hurling rocks and throwing torches.....

435   MED. CLOSE - MONSTER

       As the torches land flaming beside him, the Monster bellows his fear and quickens his stride, continuing in a PAN SHOT which shows that he crosses the road toward the marsh grass on the far side.

436   FULL SHOT

       The villagers charge after the Monster with excited:

            AD LIBS (He doesn't like fire...!
                   (Drive him into the grass...!

       The men now split into three groups. The first, headed by Toberman, continues directly toward the Monster. The other two divert to the right and left as they run toward the road, so that the only direction in which the Monster can proceed is straight ahead.

437   MED. SHOT - FROM MARSH GRASS ACROSS ROAD TOWARD VILLAGERS

       Coming toward CAMERA, the Monster plunges into the dry grass, towering above it like some mighty giant.

438   EDGE OF MARSH GRASS ON LEFT

A group of villagers headed by Schwartz run in and apply their torches to the grass. It bursts into flame.

439   EDGE OF MARSH GRASS ON RIGHT

The second group of villagers headed by Meier, are applying their torches to the grass from their side.

440   MED. SHOT - MONSTER FROM MARSH GRASS TOWARD ROAD

As the Monster comes plunging toward the CAMERA, Toberman and the others apply their torches to the grass behind him. It crackles and flames forward like a prairie fire.

441   CLOSE SHOT - MONSTER

He stops, looking with terrified eyes toward the right.

442   MARSH GRASS FROM MONSTER'S ANGLE

A wall of flame, behind which the wildly gesticulating villagers are seen, is consuming the grass ahead of it.

443   CLOSE SHOT - MONSTER

A hoarse scream of terror roars from his mouth as he looks off toward the left.

444   MARSH GRASS FROM MONSTER'S ANGLE

In front of the second group of villagers, an inferno of flame is sweeping toward the CAMERA.

445   MED. CLOSE - MONSTER

The wall of flaming grass behind him is coming closer. Again, the Monster screams his rage and fright as he plunges toward FOREGROUND.

446   IN MARSH - MED. FULL SHOT

The firmer ground ends at the edge of a muddy slough, in FOREGROUND.

As the flames hem the Monster in from three sides, he steps into the slough, wading forward in plunging steps which take him deeper and deeper into the mud.

447   MED. SHOT - FROM BEHIND TOBERMAN AND VILLAGERS,
      TOWARD MARSH

   The villagers throw whatever is at hand after the
   Monster who, with Niemann's body still under his arm,
   is seen through the wall of flame as he wades onward,
   into the slough.

448   IN MARSH - MED. FULL SHOT

   Niemann, recovering consciousness, fights wildly to free
   himself as the Monster plunges on toward the CAMERA.

   The firmer ground beneath the Monster's feet suddenly
   ends.

   A scream of terror comes from Niemann's lips as he and
   the Monster sink into the slough, until at last Niemann's
   screams are swallowed up by the mud and water, and the
   Monster - with a last snarl of terror and rage, disappears
   beneath the surface as the scene

                                        FADES OUT

                    T H E   E N D

*On the following pages we present the original Pressbook
which was distributed to theater owners
for publicity purposes.*

All Together

FRANKENSTEIN'S MONSTER!

MAD DOCTOR!

HUNCHBACK!

WOLF MAN!

DRACULA!

HOUSE OF FRANKENSTEIN

Copyright 1944, Universal Pictures Co., Inc.

New Horror Film
(Advance)

Universal's latest contribution to filmdom's Hall of Horror, "House of Frankenstein," which comes ....to the............Theatre, embodies the three most terrifying supernatural characters of fiction and drama—the Frankenstein Monster, the Wolf Man and Dracula. A vengeful scientist, portrayed by Boris Karloff, is the motivating character who resurrects these unearthly creatures, to serve his own evil purpose.

The film co-stars Karloff with Lon Chaney, and features John Carradine, J. Carrol Naish, Anne Gwynne and others.

The Cast

Doctor Niemann	Boris Karloff
Larry Talbot	Lon Chaney
Dracula	John Carradine
Rita	Anne Gwynne
Carl Hussman	Peter Coe
Arns	Lionel Atwill
Lampini	George Zucco
Ilonka	Elena Verdugo
Russman	Sig Ruman
Fejos	William Edmunds
Toberman	Charles Miller
Muller	Philip Van Zandt
Hertz	Julius Tannen
Meier	Hans Herbert
Born	Dick Dickinson
Gerlach	George Lynn
Strauss	Michael Mark
Hoffman	Olaf Hytten
Ullman	Frank Reicher
Dr. Geissler	Brandon Hurst
MONSTER	Glenn Strange

and
J. Carrol Naish as *Daniel*

Credits

Universal Pictures
Presents
"HOUSE OF FRANKENSTEIN"
Starring
BORIS KARLOFF • LON CHANEY
with
JOHN CARRADINE, J. CARROL NAISH, Anne Gwynne, Peter Coe, Elena Verdugo, Lionel Atwill
Screen Play by......Edward T. Lowe
Based on a Story by....Curt Siodmak
Director of Photography, George Robinson, A.S.C.; Art Direction, John B. Goodman, Martin Obzina; Musical Score and Direction by H. J. Salter; Director of Sound, Bernard B. Brown; Technician, William Hedgcock; Set Decorations, Russell A. Gausman, A. J. Gilmore; Film Editor, Philip Cahn; Gowns, Vera West; Assistant Director, William Tummel; Special Photography, John P. Fulton, A.S.C.
Directed by............Erle C. Kenton
Produced by............Paul Malvern

A UNIVERSAL PICTURE

Boris Karloff Menacing In New Super-Shock Film
(Advance)

In addition to his multiple screen, radio and stage interests, Boris Karloff is preparing for publication an anthology of the world's finest terror and horror literature. Having successfully compiled and edited a similar anthology, "The World's Tales of Terror," which has gone into four printings since late last year, Karloff has been commissioned by his publishers to issue a second book in the same field, but of broader scope in selection of material.

Whereas the first publication contained 15 short stories strictly on "terror" lines, his next anthology will incorporate complete short stories, passages from novels and poetry of both "terror" and "horror" category.

In the forthcoming anthology, he plans to use a portion of the Bram Stoker novel, "Dracula," upon which were based the Bela Lugosi stage play and the Universal films, "Dracula" and "Son of Dracula."

The Dracula character, a legendary giant-sized bat vampire, capable of assuming human form and draining the blood of human victims, will be brought to the screen for the third time in Karloff's current motion picture, "House of Frankenstein," in which he is co-starred with Lon Chaney, and which is due ....at the ....Theatre.

This is the Universal production which makes a bid for an all-time high in treatment of supernatural elements by bringing together Dracula (John Carradine), the Wolf Man (Lon Chaney), the Frankenstein Monster (Glenn Strange) and a newly-created character, a psychopathic hunchback murderer (J. Carrol Naish), which is reminiscent of some of the original Lon Chaney film characterizations some twenty years ago.

Karloff, who divides stellar billing with Chaney in "House of Frankenstein," appears as a vengeful scientist, who is a professed admirer of the late and unlamented Henry Frankenstein, and who seeks to continue the Frankenstein experiments to restore life in the dead.

In "House of Frankenstein"

HOUSE OF FRANKENSTEIN (2C)
Universal's thrill-film, "House of Frankenstein," co-stars Boris Karloff as the mad scientist and Lon Chaney as the Wolf Man; John Carradine appears as Dracula; J. Carrol Naish as the hunchback; Glenn Strange as the Monster. The terror-stricken girl is Elena Verdugo.

Lon Chaney's "Wolf Man" Seen Again in New Film
(Advance)

While scores of American farms are feeling the pinch of the manpower shortage, "Farmer" Lon Chaney isn't pessimistic about finding hired hands for his new 1300-acre cattle ranch in Northern California. The actor has two sons, both of whom have proven capabilities as farm hands, and pitch in after school and during their holidays.

Lon, III, 15 (his dad, the actor, is Lon, II), is 6 feet tall and weighs 175 pounds and ran a caterpillar tractor and a baler on a San Diego ranch last summer, doing the chores of two men.

The younger boy, Ron, 13, is an excellent hunter. He's the "Chaney" of the family, in his father's opinion, while Lon junior is the "thinker and worker." Both boys, obviously, have inherited their fondness for outdoor life from Lon senior, and their late grandfather, the original Lon Chaney, who used to take them on hunting trips.

Chaney's newest Universal thriller, "House of Frankenstein," in which he once again portrays the Wolf Man, is due ....at the ....Theatre. This is the third time Chaney is seen as that character. Co-starred with him is Boris Karloff as the mad scientist who brings back to life not only the Wolf Man, but Dracula and Frankenstein's Monster, as well. John Carradine portrays Dracula and Glenn Strange will be seen as the Monster, the role originally created by Karloff.

Others in the cast are J. Carrol Naish, Anne Gwynne, Peter Coe, Elena Verdugo and Lionel Atwill.

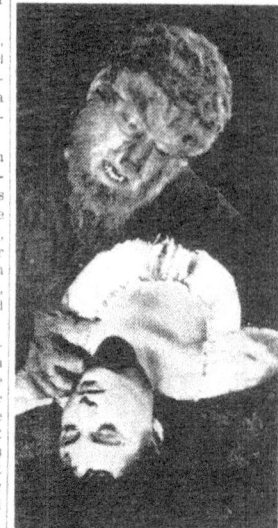

HOUSE OF FRANKENSTEIN (1C)
THE WOLF MAN, Lon Chaney, and his prey, lovely Elena Verdugo, in a thrilling scene from Universal's super-shocker, "House of Frankenstein," which co-stars Chaney and Boris Karloff.

Synopsis
(Not for Publication)

Imprisoned for 15 years because of macabre scientific experiments, Dr. Gustav Niemann (**BORIS KARLOFF**) makes his escape to freedom with Daniel (**J. CARROL NAISH**), psychopathic hunchback killer.

The unholy pair find refuge with Professor Bruno Lampini (**GEORGE ZUCCO**) in his traveling chamber of horrors. When Lampini refuses to do their bidding, Daniel throttles him and Niemann takes over.

Among the eerie exhibits in the show is the skeleton of Dracula, the human vampire (**JOHN CARRADINE**). Niemann removes the stake from the skeleton's heart, and the bones assume living form. The vampire falls in with a plan of revenge against three men responsible for Niemann's imprisonment.

Dracula casts a supernatural spell over Rita (**ANNE GWYNNE**), daughter-in-law of one of Niemann's enemies. On the verge of her transformation into a bat vampire, Rita is rescued by her husband, Carl (**PETER COE**), who destroys Dracula.

Niemann cruelly murders his enemies and with Daniel continues to the ruins of the laboratory where Frankenstein experimented on the dead. Enroute they rescue a Gypsy dancer, Ilonka (**ELENA VERDUGO**), mistreated by her master, and take her with them.

Niemann and Daniel discover the frozen forms of the Wolf Man and the man-made Frankenstein Monster buried in coffins of ice. The Wolf Man responds to heat treatments and becomes a living man, but the Monster does not.

Larry Talbot, the Wolf Man (**LON CHANEY**) helps Niemann search the wreckage of the laboratory for Frankenstein's personal diary. In it they hope to learn the secret of destroying Larry's werewolf curse.

Niemann postpones operating on Larry's brain, to continue his experiments on the Frankenstein Monster (**GLENN STRANGE**). Desperate, Larry attacks the scientist, just as the Monster shows life.

To Ilonka's horror, Larry, the man she loves, changes into the Wolf Man and smashes into her room. As his fangs sink into her neck, she kills him with the gun he had given her to protect herself against him.

Attracted by eerie lights from the Frankenstein castle, a posse of villagers destroy the Monster and the already prostrate Niemann.

Home Towns, Birth Dates

Boris Karloff	Dulwich, England	Nov. 23
Lon Chaney	Oklahoma City, Okla.	Feb. 10
John Carradine	New York, N. Y.	Feb. 5
J. Carrol Naish	New York, N. Y.	Jan. 21
Anne Gwynne	Waco, Texas	Dec. 10
Peter Coe	Dubrovnik, Jugoslavia	Nov. 11
Elena Verdugo	Paso Robles, Calif.	April 20
Lionel Atwill	London, England	March 1

PUBLICITY

"House of Frankenstein" Is Sensational Thriller
(Review)

If you're one of the vast number of thrill-film fans, you're going to get triple your money's worth when you see Universal's "House of Frankenstein," which opened yesterday at the .... Theatre. Among those present in the super-shocker are the Frankenstein Monster, Dracula and the Wolf Man—as blood-curdling a trio as was ever created.

In addition, there is a fiendish scientist, played by that master of menace, Boris Karloff, and also a hunchback with a mania for killing, portrayed convincingly and chillingly by J. Carrol Naish.

The story concerns the exploits of the scientist, who exhumes the ghoulish creatures from their graves and causes them to create havoc and terror beyond anything imaginable. Karloff, as the scientist, delivers a performance unsurpassed by anything he has yet done in his multiple activities on screen, stage and radio.

Co-starred with Karloff is Lon Chaney, who re-creates the Wolf Man, a character he has already twice portrayed.

John Carradine raises many goose pimples on his own account as Dracula, the cadaverous vampire bat, who lives by the blood of human beings. And the Frankenstein Monster, played by Glenn Strange, is enough to scare you right out of your seat.

On the more human side of the ledger are Anne Gwynne and Peter Coe, as a happily married couple who run into difficulties when Dracula enters their lives; Elena Verdugo, a Gypsy dancer, who loves the Wolf Man; Lionel Atwill, a police inspector; and George Zucco and Sig Ruman, victims of Karloff's lust for vengeance.

The film was produced by Paul Malvern from a screenplay by Edward T. Lowe, who claims that the Dracula and werewolf legends are still current in remote corners of the globe.

Earle C. Kenton's direction is excellent.

Lovely Latin Is a Blonde
(Current)

Vivacious Elena Verdugo had the unusual experience of working for the first time upon soil that once belonged to her forefathers. Universal Studio, where Miss Verdugo enacted a Gypsy dancer in "House of Frankenstein," which is now at the .... Theatre with co-stars Boris Karloff and Lon Chaney, is a portion of the original California land parcel granted by the crown of Spain to Jose Maria Verdugo, a former soldier in the Spanish Army and a lineal ancestor of luscious Elena.

Born in Paso Robles, Calif., Elena inherited not only a name illustrious in the state's history, but the warmly vivid coloring of her Castilian progenitors.

Because of the brunette cast of her complexion and her flashing eyes, Miss Verdugo has been typed in her brief but promising screen career as a Latin, despite the fact of her glowing gold blonde hair. This golden hair she has concealed for her film roles under a dark wig.

Hollywood predicts that Elena is destined for a bright future not only for her photogenic appeal, but for her ability as an actress and Spanish dancer, as well.

Boris Karloff "Terror" Film
(Current)

That old smoothie of the spine-chillers, Boris Karloff, has a bone to pick with all those who think he makes "horror" films.

The Master of Menace claims the word "horror," as applied to his type of screen and stage fare, is strictly a misnomer. The right word, he argues, is "terror."

"Horror," says the actor, "implies abhorrence, aversion and repugnance. Terror makes your hair stand on end. I don't play roles that are revolting or repulsive. Nor is 'House of Frankenstein,' my new picture, revolting or repulsive, although it is certainly destined to take the curl out of anyone's hair."

"House of Frankenstein," Universal's **terror** picture, is now at the .... Theatre, with Karloff co-starred with Lon Chaney. John Carradine and J. Carrol Naish add something extra to the film in the way of . . . you guessed it . . . terror. Others in the film are Anne Gwynne, Peter Coe, Elena Verdugo and Lionel Atwill.

She's at the Mercy of Madmen

HOUSE OF FRANKENSTEIN (2A)
BORIS KARLOFF and J. CARROL NAISH ponder the fate of Elena Verdugo in Universal's super-chiller, "House of Frankenstein," which boasts the combined menace of Dracula, the Wolf Man and Frankenstein's Monster. The film was produced by Paul Malvern.

Young Actor's Third Picture
(Current)

Wars have been more than commonplace milestones in the life of film actor Peter Coe.

He was born on a date of historic significance—Armistice Day, 1918—in Jugoslavia.

Recently, young Coe interrupted a promising screen career to enter another war, on the side of his adopted country, the United States, to which he took an oath of allegiance some time ago.

On the eve of his induction, the personable leading man finished his third film for Universal Studio, "House of Frankenstein," now at the .... Theatre. In it he shares the romantic interest with Anne Gwynne.

His first two films were "Gung Ho!" and the Technicolor "Gypsy Wildcat."

Coe came to the attention of film scouts when he appeared in the Broadway stage hit, "My Sister Eileen," in which he worked for over two years.

John Carradine's Plans Include Stage Repertory
(Current)

John Carradine, the cadaverous-looking Dracula of Universal's new thriller, "House of Frankenstein," which is now at the .... Theatre, between pictures devotes himself to Shakespearean repertory.

One of the few actors whose temperament and range fit him for both the legitimate theatre and the screen, Carradine hopes some day to establish himself and his beautiful, blonde fiancee, Sonia Sorel, as a leading stage team, similar to Alfred Lunt and Lynn Fontanne.

However, the actor wants to get several more pictures under his belt before returning to the footlights and, judging by the great demands made upon him by film producers, his departure for permanent stage work will not be too immediate.

In "House of Frankenstein," Carradine is in some excellent spine-chilling company. Boris Karloff and Lon Chaney are co-starred as a mad scientist and the Wolf Man, respectively. J. Carrol Naish is seen as a psychopathic hunchback killer and Glenn Strange appears as the Frankenstein Monster. For the lighter moments there are Anne Gwynne, Peter Coe and Elena Verdugo. Earle C. Kenton directed.

What a Cadaver
(Current)

You can be dead, and still earn $50 a week as a motion picture actor.

That's what Producer Paul Malvern paid a skeleton with the artistic mien of the late and unmourned Count Dracula, Universal's all-star shiver classic, "House of Frankenstein," now at the .... Theatre.

Rented from a company which furnishes all sorts of unusual props to the studios, the actor-cadaver contributes a highly creditable performance, too.

He was an amiable fellow to work with, claimed Director Erle C. Kenton. Took direction perfectly, didn't display an iota of temperament, and worked without stopping for lunch.

But what a ham! Without moving a single bone of his lean frame, he stole scene after scene from Boris Karloff, Lon Chaney, J. Carrol Naish, among others.

Mrs. Karloff Isn't Scared
(Advance)

If Boris Karloff is a criterion, the secret of marital happiness in Hollywood, is to be the screen's number one bogey-man.

Karloff, now increasing his professional infamy by a typically sinister role in Universal's "House of Frankenstein," and his wife observed their fourteenth wedding anniversary recently.

A devoted husband and father, the actor has a five-year-old daughter, Sara Jane, born on the star's fifty-first birthday. The child is totally unaware that her father has earned a tidy fortune by his genius for scaring people. The only movies she has been taken to see to date have been the cartoon fantasies, "Dumbo" and "Bambi."

Sara Jane doesn't even know that her father is an actor, but having been informed that he works in a place called a "studio," she frequently asks him: "When is that man going to give you a day off?"

"House of Frankenstein," co-stars Karloff with Lon Chaney, and is due .... at the .... Theatre, with John Carradine, J. Carrol Naish, Anne Gwynne. The picture re-creates Frankenstein's Monster, Dracula and the Wolf Man, plus new thrills, too.

Marked Pair

HOUSE OF FRANKENSTEIN (1B)
ANNE GWYNNE and PETER COE, lovers of Universal's "House of Frankenstein," face the menace of the mad scientist, the psychopathic hunchback, Dracula, the Wolf Man and the Monster—all in the film.

MADMAN, WOLF MAN, DRACULA, HUNCHBACK, MONSTER ... *Together!*

HOUSE OF FRANKENSTEIN (1F)
BORIS KARLOFF as the mad scientist in Universal's super-thriller, "House of Frankenstein."

HOUSE OF FRANKENSTEIN (1D)
LON CHANEY re-creates the Wolf Man in "House of Frankenstein," Universal's sensational thriller.

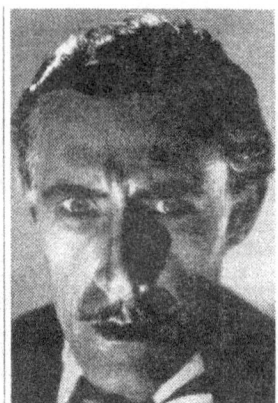
HOUSE OF FRANKENSTEIN (1G)
JOHN CARRADINE is seen as Dracula in Universal's thrill-packed horror film, "House of Frankenstein."

HOUSE OF FRANKENSTEIN (1A)
J. CARROL NAISH portrays a psychopathic hunchback in Universal's "House of Frankenstein."

HOUSE OF FRANKENSTEIN (1E)
GLENN STRANGE plays Frankenstein's Monster in Universal's exciting "House of Frankenstein."

Boris Karloff Appears As Madman in New Film
(Current)

Boris Karloff has no patience with members of his craft who deliberately turn down screen or radio offers, because the additional income would place them in a higher tax bracket.

"Actors who won't accept a picture assignment because they claim they can keep only ten per cent of the salary for themselves—the balance going to the government—are unpatriotic," he asserts.

"Certainly there's very little money sticking to one's fingers these days, because most of it goes into taxes, but that's the way it should be! We should pay for the war as we go along."

Karloff's combined income from his motion pictures, his lengthy run in the stage show, "Arsenic and Old Lace," and his radio work, indubitably add up to a very sizable total—with probably a maximum percentage assigned to the internal revenue collector.

Although he has not taken a vacation in four years, the English-born star accepted a two-picture deal at Universal Studio this year. He went from a starring role in "The Climax" immediately into a top spot in "House of Frankenstein," the super-horror spectacle which is now at the .... Theatre, with Lon Chaney his co-star.

Supporting Karloff and Chaney in the film, which marks the return of the Frankenstein Monster, the Wolf Man, Dracula and other harbingers of evil to the screen, are John Carradine, J. Carrol Naish and Anne Gwynne.

Frozen Monster.
(Current)

Glenn Strange, who is seen as the Frankenstein Monster in Universal's "House of Frankenstein," at the .... Theatre, as a boy used to explore the eerie ice caverns of his native Carlsbad, New Mexico, before they were "discovered" by the public.

It is a coincidence that as the monster in the horror film, Strange is exhumed by Boris Karloff from a subterranean ice cavern underneath Frankenstein's laboratory.

Karloff is co-starred in the super thriller with Lon Chaney.

Anne Gwynne In Thrill-Film
(Current)

Lovely, copper-haired Anne Gwynne is living proof of the fact that a small town girl can come to Hollywood, live in a whirl of adulation and publicity for five years, and still remain an unspoiled charmer.

Anne would rather waltz than jitterbug; she doesn't smoke, and that not because of the recent cigarette shortage; she doesn't drink; and she has been going with the same boy friend for two years!

Film fans have never seen Miss Gwynne pictured in movie magazines, luxuriously breakfasting in bed. A bed tray, in her home, is utilized only when a member of the family is too ill to walk.

Anne's newest film is Universal's super-thriller, "House of Frankenstein," now at the .... Theatre. In it she is surrounded by such arch villains as Boris Karloff, Lon Chaney, John Carradine and J. Carrol Naish. But Peter Coe romantically protects her.

Sissy Stuff
(Current)

Boris Karloff, whose diabolical conniving spreads a trail of blood over considerable footage of his current Universal film, "House of Frankenstein," at the .... Theatre, drinks a quart of milk daily.

The Master of Mystery and Menace is trying to gain weight!

Lon Chaney's Monster Garb
(Current)

The Frankenstein Monster garb which Glenn Strange wears in "House of Frankenstein," now at the .... Theatre, is the same worn by Lon Chaney when he played the awesome creature in "The Ghost of Frankenstein" several years ago.

As Chaney and Strange are virtually of the same height and build, Strange donned the black suit, built-up boots and other accoutrements of the Monster, without alterations.

Both men are six feet, four inches tall, and broad of shoulder. Chaney weighs 220 pounds, Strange 218.

Previous "Monsters" have included Boris Karloff and Bela Lugosi, the former introducing the character in the original Frankenstein picture filmed by Universal Studios in 1931.

"House of Frankenstein," produced by Paul Malvern, is the sixth screen appearance of the Monster, and also features the Wolf Man and Dracula, portrayed by Lon Chaney and John Carradine. Boris Karloff is starred with Chaney and is seen as the mad scientist who resurrects the horror creatures.

Lucky Actors
(Current)

Because the macabre cast corralled for Universal's "House of Frankenstein," now at the .... Theatre, was reluctant to enter the studio commissary in their horrific makeups, they assembled in Lon Chaney's dressing room for their mid-day meal, prepared by the host himself.

The incongruous gathering consisted of Boris Karloff, the sinister scientist of the picture; J. Carrol Naish, in hunchback garb; Glenn Strange, a ghoulish, eight-foot Frankenstein Monster; John Carradine as Dracula and Chaney himself in the terrifying Wolf Man characterization.

As Chaney cooks with a George Rector touch, playing screen monsters paid off in more ways than in coin of the realm.

Realist J. Carrol Naish Studies His Counterpart
(Current)

J. Carrol Naish is an actor who goes to great lengths for realism. Absorbing local color, preceding every screen role, is a habit with him, and he did not depart from custom before undertaking his current assignment, that of a hunchback psychopathic killer in "House of Frankenstein," Universal's super-thriller now at the .... Theatre, with Boris Karloff and Lon Chaney co-starred.

Naish nosed about in Los Angeles until he found a hunchback derelict to suit his purpose. He bought the fellow a hearty dinner and then fraternized around for two days, while he studied his new companion's walk and gestures.

To get a thorough perspective on how the deformed man lived, in a lodging house.

"Then," Naish said, telling Director Erle C. Kenton about the incident, "I paid a month's rent for the hunchback in a clean, moderate-class hotel and advised him to keep on taking baths."

"House of Frankenstein" re-creates three of the screen's most macabre characters—Frankenstein's Monster, Dracula and the Wolf Man.

Wolf Man, played by Glenn Strange, John Carradine and Chaney, respectively.

Please Note

The Army Overseas Motion Picture Service is exhibiting Universal's "House of Frankenstein" to service men.

In the Power of His Victims

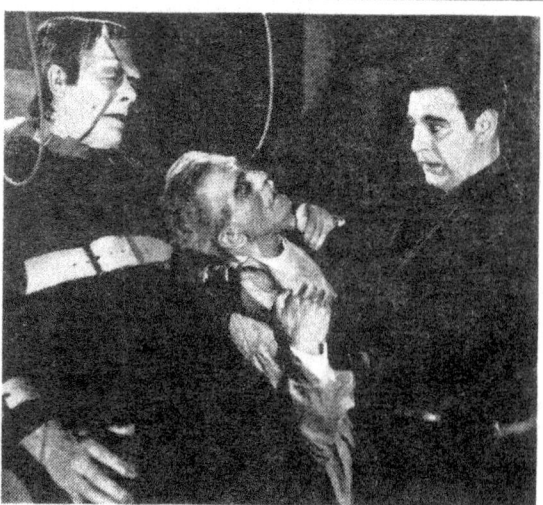
HOUSE OF FRANKENSTEIN (2B)
BORIS KARLOFF as the mad scientist of Universal's super-thriller, "House of Frankenstein," is trapped by the Wolf Man (Lon Chaney) and the Monster (Glenn Strange). Dracula is in the film, too.

SHADOW BOX

LOBBY "CHILL-TESTER"

Put the old temperature rising gag into reverse to determine the horror reaction of the picture by an easy-to-make "chill-tester" as illustrated. Copy should read: "WHAT IS YOUR CHILL REACTION? ...HOW MUCH CAN YOU TAKE?...YOUR BLOOD WILL TURN TO ICE WHEN YOU SEE THE YEAR'S TOP THRILL SHOW "HOUSE OF FRANKENSTEIN" WITH FIVE FAMOUS HORROR CHARACTERS ...ETC."

Giant "thermometer" carries the copy as indicated in the illustration "Normal, Cool, Cold, Frigid, Zero and You Have Icewater in Your Veins." It is designed so that temperature fluid drops when a patron steps on the platform. Large glass tube with rubber hose connecting it with ordinary hot-water bottle are the necessary props. Set up is shown in detail in the diagram below sketch. Person stepping on platform releases pressure on hot-water bottle, allowing fluid to recede in tube.

FRIGHT INSURANCE

Set up an advance insurance booth in your foyer to issue "Fright Insurance" to all patrons. A deal might be made with a local live-wire insurance man to handle the stunt in return for personal publicity. Use the "policies" as give-aways.

Print "gag" policies (to look like the real thing) with the "fright" clause worded something like this: "The person named below will be entitled to free admittance to another showing of the "HOUSE OF FRANKENSTEIN" if sufficient evidence is presented to the management that he or she missed any portion of said show by reason of having fainted through fright."

ORDER YOUR TRAILER EARLY
from your local
NATIONAL SCREEN SERVICE

FIRST AID FOR SHOCK

This time-honored stunt of a "First Aid for Shock" booth should be taken from your files and dusted off for this picture. Have a white garbed "nurse" in attendance at all times. Build a board to hold the following items: Cotton Pads . . . "to keep knees from knocking". False Teeth . . . "for those who swallow their own in the excitement." Chewing Gum . . . "to keep teeth from chattering." Wool Socks . . . "in case of cold feet." Safety Belt . . . "to keep you in your chair." Electric Heating Pad . . . "for cold shivers." Smelling Salts . . . "in case of severe shock." Hair Dye . . . "for those whose hair turns white." Hospital Phone Number . . . "in case of emergency" etc.

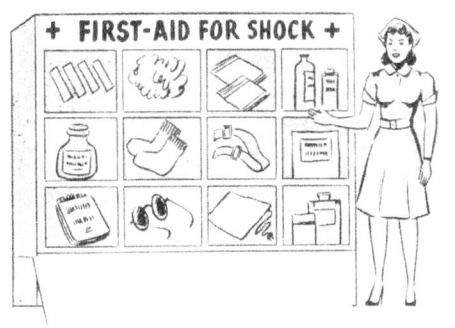

A little time and effort expended on your one sheet and you will have a socko seat-selling advance shadow-box for your lobby. Illustrated are the units, how to cut them out and use them to the best advantage in this display. Build your shadow box in the usual way and paint black inside. Mount the figure of the girl across the front. On a separate plane half way back in the box use the cut-out figure of the Frankenstein Monster together with his shadow. Arrange all five "horror heads" across the top of box and finish off with your title and display line (as shown). Illuminate in greens and blues with a flasher on spot covering the "monster".

SHOCK PREVENTION

USE CIRCUS BARKER WITH HORROR EXHIBITS

"HISS VILLAIN" CONTEST

A natural for lobby ballyhoo of the famous horror characters to be found in "HOUSE OF FRANKENSTEIN" is the lobby "barker" of the circus variety. Have your man dressed in the typical checked suit and derby hat and stand him on a box surrounded by blow-ups of the horror characters. Mount your blow-ups on sign cloth banners.

Barker would, of course, spiel about the "greatest collection of horror characters ever gathered together on one screen . . . see the devastating Frankenstein Monster . . . Hear the hideous wild cry of the Wolf-Man . . . feel the hypnotic influence of Dracula . . . stand aghast at the terror caused by the Mad Doctor and the Hunchback . . . etc."

TRICK PASS GAG

Don't PASS up "House of Frankenstein"
Use this FREE invitation plus a regular ticket of admission for
FIVE-PLY HORROR THRILLS
RIVOLI THEATRE

A trick card could be printed (to appear like a pass) and handed out by your lobby circus barker. Some takers would pass the gag along, asking a friend if he wanted a "pass" to the show, as on first sight the card should look like one of your legitimate passes.

SHOCK TEST MACHINE

Your local coin machine concessionaire will probably have one of these familiar little machines. Locate one and spot it in your lobby. Machine has a lever which when turned (or gripped hard enough) gives a slight harmless electrical shock to the user. Stunt is well adapted to this picture due to the fact that FIVE, instead of one, horror characters are present. Here is suggested copy for card over machine: CHECK YOUR SHOCK RESISTANCE HERE. Test yourself. Can you stand the five ply shock awaiting you when you see "HOUSE OF FRANKENSTEIN"?

All theatre-goers like to "hiss" the villain. Instead of only ONE villain to hiss "HOUSE OF FRANKENSTEIN" has FIVE. This fact opens wide a chance to gather a poll from your patrons as to which character they "hate" the most. Conduct a "HISS THE VILLAIN CONTEST" in your lobby.

Such a contest, started at least a week in advance of your playdates, will start seat-selling interest and talk around town. Set up a regulation ballot-box in your lobby. Carry this banner copy across the top: "HISS THE VILLAIN CONTEST . . . VOTE FOR THE HORROR CHACTER YOU HATE THE MOST!" On one side of the display place a board with the heads of each character, The Mad Doctor, the Frankenstein Monster, the Wolf Man, the Hunchback and Dracula.

Prepare "Shock Prevention" give-aways by using the ordinary small glassine "window" envelope containing two or three pieces of hard candy (small ones that look like pills). Imprint the front of the envelope with: "*PROTECT YOURSELF AGAINST FIVE-PLY SHOCK*" . . . "*take these shock-prevention pills as an antidote for the shock in store for you when you see the Mad Doctor, the Frankenstein Monster, the Wolf-Man, the Hunchback and Dracula ALL TOGETHER in "HOUSE OF FRANKENSTEIN" at the RIVOLI theatre.*" Make one envelope for each character as shown.

A tie-up can be made with your nearest local druggist for the needed candy "pills". Have the envelopes imprinted on the back with: "*FOR YOUR DAILY PRITECTION ALWAYS TRADE WITH BLANK DRUGGISTS FOR . . . ETC.*"

LOBBY LIGHTING

In order to effect an eerie atmosphere in your lobby place several green and blue spots at strategic corners (near the floor) so that patrons walking through the lobby will throw huge, flitting shadows across the lobby walls. The same idea applies to shadows from any cut-out standees of the horror characters you might have on display.

Free Radio Transcriptions

The air lanes offer a real socko medium for selling the horror angle of "HOUSE OF FRANKENSTEIN." Go after the horror fans with this special radio transcription! Spot it before and after the well known scare shows on the air and you have advertising value that's hard to beat!

Here's a suggestion for a real effect in your campaign. Have local announcer read short single sentence messages in a weird, foreboding voice at various intervals throughout the day using this type of copy . . . *LISTEN IN TONIGHT, AT (GIVE TIME) IF YOU'VE GOT THE NERVE! IT CONCERNS THE "HOUSE OF FRANKENSTEIN"*

. . . You can use the ghostly, mysterious laugh which you'll find scattered throughout the transcription. You can build up a lot of valuable enthusiasm with this type of teaser campaign. The pressings are on "Vinolite" the material which guarantees perfect fidelity in radio broadcasting.

We feel that these recordings will add a great deal to the strength of your advertising campaign, and go a long way in solving your radio problems. There are six station breaks, two half minute announcements, and two full minute spots. Ample time has been allowed for local announcer to give theatre name and play date. This transcription is FREE! Send for it now!

WRITE, WIRE OR PHONE

EXPLOITATION DEP'T
UNIVERSAL PICTURES CO., INC.
UNIVERSAL CITY, CALIFORNIA

DESCRIPTION: All heads in full color against a green-blue background. Title in green with yellow highlights. Cast in white.

SIX SHEET

ONE SHEET

THREE SHEET

14x36

22x28

MIDGET AND REGULAR WINDOW CARDS

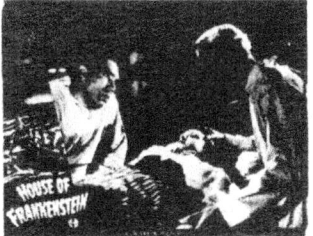
SET OF EIGHT 11x14s

ORDER ALL ACCESSORIES FROM YOUR LOCAL NATIONAL SCREEN SERVICE EXCHANGE

Ad No. 107—1 Col. Mat 15c

Ad No. 106—1 Col. Mat 15c

Ad No. 208—2 Col. Mat 30c

Ad No. 203—2 Col. Mat 30c

Ad No. 205—2 Col. Mat 30c

Ad No. 206—2 Col. Mat 30c

Ad No. 104—1 Col. Mat 15c

ALL THE SCREEN'S MONSTERS OF TERROR...

TOGETHER...

in the Greatest sensation of **ALL TIME!**

WOLF MAN!

FRANKENSTEIN'S MONSTER!

DRACULA!

MAD DOCTOR!

HUNCHBACK!

HOUSE OF FRANKENSTEIN

starring
BORIS KARLOFF   **LON CHANEY**
with
JOHN CARRADINE   **J. CARROL NAISH**

ANNE GWYNNE   PETER COE
ELENA VERDUGO   LIONEL ATWILL

ADDED ATTRACTIONS

Screen Play by Edward T. Lowe · Directed by ERLE C. KENTON · A UNIVERSAL PICTURE · Produced by PAUL MALVERN · Based on a Story by Curt Siodmak

Ad No. 501—5 Col. Mat 75c

The editor gratefully acknowledges the assistance and contributions provided by the following individuals in the preparation of this series over the past 20 years:

Bud Abbott (Late)
Patty Andrews
Evelyn Ankers
Lew Ayres
William Bakewell
Ralph Bellamy
Stanley Bergerman
Robert Bloch
Richard Bojarski
Lincoln Bond
Ronald Borst
David Bradley
Kevin Brownlow
Ivan Butler
James Cagney (Late)
John Carradine (Late)
Ben & Anne Carre
Jeffrey Carrier
Ronald Chaney
Lon Chaney Jr. (Late)
Carlos Clarens (Late)
Mae Clarke
Peter Coe
Franklin Coen
Ned Comstock
Mary Corliss
James Curtis
Nancy Cushing-Jones
Robert Cushman
Walter Daugherty
Gary Dorst
Todd Feiertag
Bramwell Fletcher (Late)
Robert Florey (Late)
A. Arnold Gillespie (Late)
Curtis Harrington
Patricia Hitchcock
Valerie Hobson
Bob Hope
David S. Horsley (Late)
Henry Hull (Late)
Paul Ivano (Late)
Steven Jochsberger (Late)
Zita Johann
Raymond F. Jones
Boris Karloff (Late)
John Kobal
Carl Laemmle Jr.
Carla Laemmle
Elsa Lanchester (Late)
John Landis
Janet Leigh
Celia Lovsky
Arthur Lubin
Rouben Mamoulian (Late)
Paul Mandell
Howard Mandlebaum
Gregory Mank
David Manners
Lester Matthews
John McLaughlin
Scott McQueen
Patsy Ruth Miller
Jeff Morrow
Gary Pasternak
Jim Pepper
Anthony Perkins
Mary Philbin
Armando Ponce
Vincent Price
Dr. Donald Reed
William Rosar
Margaret Ross
Hans J. Salter
Anne Schlosser
Martin Scorsese
Sherry Seeling
Wes Shank
Curt Siodmak
Robert Skotak
Joseph Stephano
James Stewart
Glenn Strange (Late)
Kenneth Strickfaden (Late)
George Turner
Edward Van Sloan (Late)
Elena Verdugo
Marc Wanamaker
Dan Woodruff
Wallace Worsley Jr.
and
FORREST J ACKERMAN, Founder of the Ackerman Archives. During the early 30s, FJA had exchanged 62 letters with Carl Laemmle Sr. As a result, Mr. Laemmle on his President's stationery, wrote a note to whom it may concern saying, in effect, "Give this young man anything he wants." As a consequence, the young Forry Ackerman acquired stills, posters, pressbooks, and the sound discs from FRANKENSTEIN, THE MUMMY, THE OLD DARK HOUSE and MURDERS IN THE RUE MORGUE. Since that date, the collection has grown to hundreds of thousands of items dealing with the classic Universal films, and items from the Science Fiction and Fantasy genre. We are indeed fortunate to have this wonderland of memorabilia as our foundation. Nearly 60 years later, almost to the word, Universal Studios has granted Philip J. Riley, one of Ackerman's former assistants, and MagicImage Filmbooks the same gift in recognition of their concern and realization of Universal's great heritage in the art of Motion Picture Production. Combined with the talents and contributions of those named above, we pledge to produce the highest quality historic works, so that future generations may benefit from firsthand knowledge of the magical city of Hollywood which created a new art form - and unknowingly protected the greatest gift of our childhood - the imagination.